MW00423143

Praise for *Go!*

"Tired of pretzeling yourself into a career and work world that doesn't work for you? *Go!: Reboot Your Career in 90 Days* helps you redesign your life and provide the hope, help, and community you need to flourish. Whether you're looking for more autonomy, purpose, or impact from your work, Lisa Thee gives you the career reboot actions to redefine success on your own terms and to take the big leap of making that success a reality."

—**David Smith and Brad Johnson,** *New York Times* best-selling authors of *Good Guys: How Men Can Be Better Allies for Women in the Workplace*

"Compelling and inspirational, Lisa distills her life experience and shares the success formula for navigating today's world of work on your own terms. Her 90-day career reboot plan is a roadmap for women seeking a more fulfilling work and life."

—**Amii Barnard-Bahn,** best-selling author of *The PI Guidebook: How the Promotability Index® Can Help You Get Ahead in Your Career* and named a Top 25 Coaching Thought Leader by Thinkers360

"With *Go!*, Lisa provides an original, personal, yet very accurate analysis of the modern work equation. She has the courage to propose new standards for the way we should look at work that kill the "workaholic" model and propose a much healthier path for the best work life. Lisa identifies the main ingredients of the modern work life recipe: work ethics, diversity and inclusion, empathy, emotional intelligence, and self-care, just to mention a few, and articulates them around a magical formula anyone can learn from. With vulnerability and in a very humble way, Lisa illustrates some of the principles she's building her approach on through examples from her own life. *Go!* balances those personal inputs with general advice that's easy to act upon, making the book a clear must-read for anyone who is willing to rethink their relationship with work and make the right choices to align their work with their purpose."

—**Kévin Bouchareb,** director of future of work and human resources strategy at Ubisoft

"In *Go!*, Lisa Thee takes a unique approach to a 90-day reboot plan that will take you from a career that is on autopilot to a career that truly excites you and sparks passion. Lisa is masterful at caring for the holistic side of an individual and showing how to get out of the box and leave stagnation behind. The examples in *Go!* are real-world and inspire you to start your journey knowing the destination is achievable. Read *Go!* if you are in that place of asking the question, 'What next?'"

—**Hilary DeCesare,** transitional expert and executive coach, CEO of The ReLaunch Co., podcast and radio show host, and best-selling author of *RELAUNCH!: Spark Your Heart to Ignite Your Life*

"*Go!: Reboot Your Career in 90 Days* is a must-read for any woman in the workforce today. Lisa shares her personal story on how she redesigned her career and provides actionable steps for her readers to do the same. You will finish this book excited and empowered to create a career that is both fulfilling and impactful."

—Jamie Fiore Higgins, author of *Bully Market, My Story of Money and Misogyny at Goldman Sachs,* 2022 *Financial Times* Top 25 Women of the Year

"Whether you need to build your own 90-day reboot plan or support people in your organization to build more fulfilling careers, you'll find a wealth of resources in *Go!*"

—JeanAnn Nichols, professor at Stanford, keynote speaker, and coach for PrismWork, LLC

"*Go!: Reboot Your Career in 90 Days* by Lisa Thee is an engaging and intelligent, easy-to-read book. Lisa is an inspiration to the modern work world. She clearly outlines her path to success and the many different types of roads she traversed to get there. Her navigation through the business world despite setbacks is a true inspiration. She illuminates the way to find balance between success and holding on to personal, mission-driven values. Through her journey, Lisa guards the vulnerable and protects those that cannot protect themselves, while drawing boundaries and valuing her own peace. I highly recommend this relatable and powerful guide to expanding the notion of what is possible in your career!"

—Liz Harman, senior program manager and analyst, Blue Shield of California

"It is during moments of extreme change and chaos that we look to the trailblazers—the leaders who have traveled the journey before us—and eagerly await the breadcrumbs of knowledge they bestow. As I shift into the next chapter of my career, I found the 90-day plan actionable, informative, and insightful. I'm ready to GO!"

—**Wendy Turner-Williams,** board member, chief data officer, keynote speaker, and a member of the Top 100 Women in Technology and Global Data Power Women

Go!

Go!

Reboot Your
Career in 90 Days

LISA THEE

FC

FAST
COMPANY
Press

Fast Company Press
New York, New York
www.fastcompanypress.com

Distributed by Greenleaf Book Group

For ordering information or special discounts for bulk purchases, please contact Greenleaf Book Group at PO Box 91869, Austin, TX 78709, 512.891.6100.

Grateful acknowledgment is made to the following sources for permission to reproduce copyrighted material:
Values Exercise from the blog post "Live Your Core Values: 10-Minute Exercise to Increase Your Success," by Barb Carr. © 2013 by Aaron Hurst. Reprinted by permission of Aaron Hurst on behalf of TapRoot.

Design and composition by Greenleaf Book Group
Cover design by Greenleaf Book Group
Cover Images: ©Leremy; Stefan Balaz. Used under license from Shutterstock.com

Publisher's Cataloging-in-Publication data is available.

Print ISBN: 978-1-63908-059-5

eBook ISBN: 978-1-63908-060-1

To offset the number of trees consumed in the printing of our books, Greenleaf donates a portion of the proceeds from each printing to the Arbor Day Foundation. Greenleaf Book Group has replaced over 50,000 trees since 2007.

Printed in the United States of America on acid-free paper
23 24 25 26 27 28 29 30   10 9 8 7 6 5 4 3 2 1
First Edition

I want to thank the following people for their love and support which allows me to thrive: Garrett Thee, Tessa Thee, Brandon Thee, David Polvi, Suzanne Polvi, Lynn Fraser, Craig Fraser, Anna Miller, Colleen McClelland, Shannon Bally, Laura Gaffney, and Sara Arsenault.

Contents

Preface: Long Hauler   xiii

Author's Note   xxi

Introduction: What Has Worked Is No Longer Working   1

Part 1: Employee Headwinds   7

    Chapter 1: The Right Work Ethic   9

    Chapter 2: Vicarious Trauma   19

    Chapter 3: We All Need Self-Care   32

    Chapter 4: Post-Traumatic Wisdom   40

    Chapter 5: #MeToo; Now What?   47

    Chapter 6: InteGRITy   61

Part 2: Employer Headwinds—The Future of Work   75

    Chapter 7: How Work Has Changed for Women   77

    Chapter 8: Innovation, Impact, and Inclusion   88

    Chapter 9: Healthcare Not Sick Care   106

    Chapter 10: The Role of Male Allies   118

Part 3: Your 90-Day Career Reboot   127

    Chapter 11: The Career Reboot Process   129

Part 4: Many Ways to Go   161

    Chapter 12: Smashing Success   163

    Chapter 13: Build for Your Mission with Intrapreneurship   169

    Chapter 14: Spark Passion with Entrepreneurship   178

    Chapter 15: Follow the Yellow Brick Road   197

Remembering Hasan   203

Acknowledgments   207

Appendix: The Executive's Guide
   to Retaining Your Top Talent   209

Notes   217

About the Author   223

Long Hauler

In early January 2020, the long-awaited message finally arrived: I had been selected to give a keynote on my anti-human-trafficking work for a TEDx conference. This was a bucket-list dream of mine and far beyond what I ever thought I would achieve. Fewer than one percent of TEDx applicants are ever accepted, and this was my first application. I immediately started the process of preparing for the event, scheduled for August 2020.

Three months later, my dream turned into a nightmare. In late March, the pandemic shut down schools. At the time, I was a management consultant for Microsoft and an elementary school teacher for two children. After several months of this relentless schedule, I was on a countdown to summer break for a chance to recover from the burnout. The TEDx conference was postponed, giving me more time to prepare. But just before school let out, I started to feel *not quite right*.

xiv   Go!

Through most of June, I was showing symptoms we now know are COVID, but at the time, I didn't meet the criteria for testing, which was in very limited supply. So, I did what working parents do every day: I just got it done. The housework, the cooking, my job, the kids, and trying to find ways to break up the boredom of lockdown—I did it all. Then my husband got a cough and was able to get in for a test, which turned out positive. I was formally diagnosed the week of July 4th.

So early in the pandemic, we didn't know any other families that had tested positive. Making the phone calls to our bubble of friends and family to let them know we may have exposed them was a huge shame trigger. I was relieved when my husband seemed mostly back to normal seven days later, but my symptoms kept dragging on and on. By January 2021, I could literally no longer hold my head up after an eight-hour workday, and I had chronic fatigue that forced me back to bed by 2:00 p.m. every day. With the lockdown still in place, we were still homeschooling our kids, and my husband worked out of our bedroom. We felt like fish in a barrel, wondering if some sense of normality would return and the kids could go back to school. That March, I was diagnosed with postacute sequelae of COVID, also known as *long COVID*, and was put on medical disability with a reduced schedule while getting treatments to reduce my symptoms. The kids were back in school. Things seemed to finally start looking up.

The new date for my TEDx talk was set for August 2021. That timing felt very achievable, because I already had a good portion of my speech written back in early 2020, before I got sick and the pandemic shut everything down. I was feeling

pretty confident going into the summer that I would be prepared . . . right up until the final months, where I transitioned
from speechwriting to memorization. I did not have a diagnosis
at the time for what I would later learn was neurological impair-
ment from long COVID. My processing speed and ability to
learn new things had plummeted to the bottom 2 percent of
the population. No matter how long I practiced, I was unable
to retain my speech and was dropping large chunks of it during
my dry runs. TED is very specific about speakers not having
a teleprompter or notes on stage and will disqualify you from
speaking if they are used. Two days before my talk, I had not suc-
cessfully delivered the speech from memory even a single time.

I hit full-fledged panic mode. Thinking fast, I recorded my
dry run in two-minute increments the day before the event so
that, if I got up there and stood like a deer in headlights in front
of the audience, I could at least submit my speech to TEDx for

TEDx talk delivered!

the website instead. I was so scared that I sweated through my blazer during the dress rehearsal and had to find a new outfit the next morning to do the real thing in.

Something about having the video backup just in case helped my brain finally track, and I was extremely relieved to have my speech go off the next day without a hitch. I feel like the universe must have been looking out for me that day, and I am deeply grateful to my speechwriters, coaches, mentors, and allies for helping me deliver the speech of my life.

Despite that win, in 2022, I had a relapse of my long COVID, marked by chronic fatigue and confusion. I realized that management consulting was not a sustainable job for someone with my health condition. For a client-facing consultant, your schedule is often unpredictable, so it did not fit well with the three-days-a-week, no-more-than-four-hours-a-day restriction from my doctors. My best innovation and creativity were only available to me in the morning. When I pushed beyond my energy budget for the day, I would pay a high price the rest of the week for ignoring my body's signals. After COVID, I learned every time I overexerted myself, I had to pay it back with 40 percent interest; so, getting clear on what I was willing to spend my energy on became an urgent priority.

After one particularly long workday in January where everything that could go wrong did at home, at work, and in my medical outlook, something had to give. I found that pushing through had undone the benefit for a year of physical and occupational therapy. I was in so much pain that I was bedridden for three days straight. This was in stark contrast to my LinkedIn profile, which highlighted my recent awards as a 2022 Top 50

Global Thought Leader for AI and privacy, and my ranking as number 1 for health and safety on Thinkers360. Ironic, I know.

It was time for me to dust off my old set of tools—coping mechanisms, processes, and attitudes that I had used during my time as an executive coach helping people transition from careers that were causing them burnout to something more sustainable. I relied on low-tech solutions for the unintended consequences of an always-on culture: nature, daily walks, meditation, time with family, and, most importantly, setting boundaries. Once I drowned out the noise of the world, I was able to tune into my own body's wisdom and clarify my values, which allowed me to define a new path forward—one based on the life and legacy I wanted to have, on my own terms, where I invested my time in creating a more sustainable future for myself.

As measures of success go, these were a far cry from the goals I had chased all my life. My family, the workplace, and society prioritized record-setting productivity, one-size-fits-all work processes, and presenteeism (digital or otherwise). But I had learned through lived experience that if you don't have your health, you don't have anything. So, I took the reins of my own life and embarked on a two-year journey of researching my genetics, environment, and lab data to identify the root cause of my illness. Eventually, I was diagnosed with a serious form of vasculitis (called Behçet's disease), an underlying condition I didn't know I'd had for eleven years until COVID triggered new, diagnosable symptoms, including sleep apnea, aneurysms, sudden hearing loss, GI issues, chronic fatigue, anxiety, and brain fog.

At the same time that I was struggling with the reemergence

of my vasculitis symptoms, I noticed that the news cycle was full of stories about people losing their jobs, burning out on their careers, or becoming disabled because of COVID. I realized that I wasn't the only one who'd spent the last few years feeling like their life and career had been turned upside down by a pandemic that has had unexpected medical, social, and economic consequences for people across the globe.

Even though we were all weathering the same storm, our circumstances were not affecting everyone in the same way. It had been clear since early in the COVID-19 pandemic that our new normal was particularly debilitating for working moms, who were bearing the brunt of the invisible labor at home and at work. The term *she-cession* was making it into the zeitgeist, and within the course of a couple of years, we had set women's representation in the workplace back four decades—to 1980s levels, according to *Forbes*.[1]

In the early pandemic of 2020, people seemed to be struggling equally. Although the job market picked up again in 2021, it did so much more for men than for women. During the entire pandemic, women have been disproportionately affected. When omicron hit in 2022, those numbers separated even further: "eight hundred seventy-five thousand new jobs for men and just sixty-two thousand for women."[2]

I decided to write this book as a guide for others who, like me, for one reason or another, find themselves in the position of needing to blow up their careers and redefine success on their own terms. That can be a scary place to be, emotionally, but there is also so much potential for change, growth, and transformation. My goal is to help you redesign your life to provide you with the hope, help, and community that you need to flourish instead of chasing the traditional measures of career success that assume you either have a stay-at-home spouse to pick up all the slack or are willing to burn out from a lack of support.

"Women are even more burned out than they were a year ago," stated *Women in the Workplace 2021*, "and the gap in burnout between women and men has almost doubled." According to the report, a third of women were considering quitting or reducing their career focus in 2021, up from a quarter a year earlier.[3]

The burden of constant unbounded achievement is just too heavy to balance with family, health, and happiness on your own. Every yes you say to the world is a no you say to yourself. Let's free up your discretionary energy for the next few months and create a new way of living, one where when the next emergency rolls around, you have the ability to put your own oxygen mask on first so you can lead those who rely on you.

This book is for career leaders managing in this new environment and stymied by it themselves. Whether you're an executive at a multinational company investing in retention strategies for your top talent, a leader on the edge of burnout, or an aspiring entrepreneur who is looking to bring your own unique vision into the world, this book will guide you to creating a clear roadmap from where you are today to a more fulfilling future. Let me help you step into your power and help ensure that, as leaders, we have enough representation, creativity, and influence to create the next twenty years of products, innovations, and services that will be designed with less bias, more mission, and an inclusive mindset.

Author's Note

I've designed this book to be both illuminator and guide. The early chapters give insights into the workplace today, with career reboot actions at the end of each chapter that prime you for the 90-Day Career Reboot, but you can start at whichever point in the book that serves your needs right now. Ready to put pen to paper and plan your career reboot right now? Jump to chapter 11. Want to learn about a specific workplace issue? Skip to the chapter that covers that particular challenge. Start with the chapter you need, and enjoy this book in the order that helps you.

—

I surveyed over thirty women in 2022 on their experiences on their path to leadership and included many of their thoughts in this book. The survey participants represent a cross section of executive women: VP level and up from multi-national corporations, CEOs of private companies, entrepreneurs, and thought leaders. The goal of including their feedback is to dispel the myth that gender-based tailwinds to leadership are only personal problems. What their experiences show is that many of these problems that feel personal are often pervasive.

What Has Worked Is No Longer Working

"Overwhelm is the all-too-common feeling that our lives are somehow unfolding faster than the human nervous system and psyche are able to manage well."

—attributed to Jon Kabat-Zinn

You're probably already feeling the urge for a change in your life. Perhaps something about your current situation feels untenable or you've been yearning for more—more time, autonomy, mission, or impact from your work. Today's workplace has been optimized for productivity in every aspect, and it can sometimes feel relentless. Setting boundaries and holding to them can feel impossible at times, especially when you are working against a company culture that tolerates toxicity in leadership or where your peers are pushing themselves to burnout. Well, there is more waiting for you on the other side of your predictable, stable career. These yearnings you have are not only good; they are also what will propel you to grow as a leader, a family member, and a human. Only when we are clear on our vision for success can we maximize our full potential and start to live from a place of abundance instead of scarcity.

For the first twenty years of my career, I did all the things I was told you were "supposed" to do for lifelong success: I went to the right schools, studied engineering, took on challenging roles where I expanded my skills, and ultimately achieved an executive position at a global technology company. And I learned that following a path that was laid out for you will only lead to you fulfilling someone else's dream, whether or not that dream fulfills you. So today, I am here to amplify the restless feeling inside you, your desire to define success on your own terms and to take the big leap of making that success a reality for yourself. I hope to be your guide on a career transformation journey of your own. Let's start at the beginning, taking a closer look at how I redefined my own career and what it means to be successful in it.

FORGING AHEAD WITHOUT A COMPASS

From my rustbelt roots in the metropolitan Detroit area, my career took me west to California just months before the dot-com bust in Silicon Valley would hit the industry hard. It only took a week for this recent college graduate to decide that I *never* wanted to be an executive there, because the cost to my quality of life would be way too high. Looking back with the benefit of hindsight twenty years later, I was right. The work world was not accommodating to women, especially once they had a family. The number of microinequities around the office directed toward the people who had to leave early for school pick up or who missed another meeting because of a sick family member was ever present, and it was clear you did not want to be considered in that group come annual review time.

Searching for inspiration, I looked to the women in VP and C-suite positions—those leaders I had been trained from birth to emulate. I could not find a single role model whose lifestyle I wanted. The women I did see at the top looked exhausted, weary, and lonely. They were married to their careers. While that's a choice some women might make happily, I wasn't among them. It seemed to me that these women had to sacrifice their boundaries in order to survive in the executive world, and I was not ready to commit to that path at twenty-one years old.

My experience wasn't unique. Now, I know many women who also had difficulty envisioning what success might look like during their early careers, when no one at the leadership level was living a lifestyle that seemed worth all the blood, sweat, and tears they paid for it. The concept of work–life balance was updated to "you can have it all, just not at once." It was left to women to figure out how to manage that balance; changing the systems that they had to perform in was not part of the conversation. There was no consideration of the social supports required to realize this vision of success in an "up or out" culture. As the responsibilities of life grew outside of the office, the margins for error—and the time for sleep or self-care—diminished quickly even if there was someone else to help at home. This system assumes we will all be able bodied forever, unincumbered with caretaking responsibility, free to travel, and always willing to relocate to rise to the top of an organization.

The last five years have introduced even more challenges to the twenty-first-century working woman. Many of you live them daily. I'm not a fan of shying away from tough topics; I probably wouldn't have tried to tackle the issue of human trafficking if I was. We need to put the challenges women face today on the table and examine whether today's work models have kept pace with reality. Spoiler alert: The data on the retention of women leaders tells us there is more work to do.

This book is part validation of those experiences, part awareness for those who may not know what others face in and outside of work, and part empowerment to help define modern feminism for yourself and create the career you dream of.

YOU MUST CHANGE YOUR LIFE

"The rich invest in time; the poor invest in money."
—attributed to Warren Buffett

If you feel like you're on a treadmill going faster than you can keep up with from the moment you wake up until the moment your head hits the pillow at night, you may lack boundaries. You may already be on the edge of burnout. When you fail to set boundaries for yourself, you also fail to set priorities for yourself. As a result, your boundaries will end up being dictated by the needs of those around you. It's very easy to get lost in the urgency of other people's needs and to lose sight of your vision for your own career and life. I have learned over the years that the key to successful leadership is taking the time to clarify your values and priorities and then ensuring you follow through on them by protecting your time.

Navigating work in a post-pandemic world has created more opportunity for accountability and boundaries in the workplace. With the rise of remote or hybrid work environments, there exists much more flexibility in how we get work done. If you are ready to make a real change in your life, know that you don't need to go all-in to start. Some practices I have adopted over the years to protect my own time include figuring out what I need to work efficiently without burning out and taking the time to make those things happen. For example, I do my innovation-oriented work in the morning, when I have the most energy and before I check text messages, emails, or Slack. I take a daily walk to see the tops of the trees and the blue of the sky and to remember how small we all are in the grand scope of the world. I also turn off my computer at 5:00 p.m. during the week so I can start again the next day refreshed. You will never get to the end of your to-do list; most things can wait.

Once you get a taste of living your own mission and higher purpose, it's really hard to go back to punching a clock just for money. Your journey may keep you on your current career path or may lead you into new arenas. Life circumstances don't allow everyone to be able to quit their current job without a backup. It is possible to have a mission, financial stability, and time for rest, but some creativity and job-crafting will likely be required to make it possible in the corporate world. The important thing is to focus on what aligns with your mission and to keep doubling down on your strengths in the areas where you can do that work while making money (or else it's a hobby). As a woman playing the game in corporate America, I have found much more satisfaction bringing my whole self as a leader than trying to fit into what was expected of me from someone else's company culture.

I want to help you find that same satisfaction I've found. In this book, I'm going to share with you a process for defining success on your own terms, a guide for how to transition your career in that direction, and inspiring examples of marginalized people who have made a similar change. Success is a team sport, and I am here to help you every step of the way with encouragement, empathy, and community to bring your best self to the world, whether you decide to lead from inside an organization or go out on your own.

PART 1

Employee Headwinds

CHAPTER 1

The Right Work Ethic

*"We're totally guilty of doing too much at once, all while
trying to manage the noise in our heads that
says we are not doing enough."*
—Vanessa Autrey

My first summer job was as a production supervisor on the Cadillac engine assembly line in the 1990s. These were the days when taking a job meant choosing a side. You were either management or union. These assembly-line jobs paid well and were provided only to union employees with a high seniority status of twenty-five years or more.

Can you imagine turning the same bolt every minute, eight hours a day for twenty-five years? My father and his father before him were both members of the union, and he worked midnights as a plating chemist when I was young. Eventually, after a twenty-five-year pause before completing his degree, my father finished college and was promoted into management, retiring as the head of environmental engineering and safety at General Motors.

It piqued my curiosity to understand how people could tolerate the boredom, and I talked with the people on my production team to better understand how they did it. In the early morning hours on the second shift, I learned that everyone had a different reason for showing up and also had a different way of coping with the monotony. The answers ranged from daydreaming about their children being the first in the family to go to college all the way to figuring out how to read paperback thrillers while waiting for the production line to move a new engine to their station.

The message I was given was that it was my job, as a manager, to keep the line moving, since every minute it was down cost roughly five thousand dollars. Productivity was the measure of the day, with an interesting twist: Because it was a union environment, it was virtually impossible for anyone to be fired or promoted. That's where I learned how to lead when you don't have sticks and carrots to dangle. The key to unlocking people's innate work ethic is simple and hard at the same time. It is treating everyone with dignity and respect. The difference between the line running with seventy-five percent efficiency one night and ninety-nine percent the next was determined by the relationships you formed with your team.

Every single time the line went down, I had to page a skilled tradesperson to push a button to reset it per union contract guidelines. The first week on the job, when I made a suggestion about how to make a task easier, one worker wagged her finger in an inch from my nose and said, "I have underwear older than you. I'm not listening to a f***ing thing you say."

After a couple of months and many hours of getting to know my team on a deeper level, they often would offer to push the button to reset the machine for me themselves. Given that the plant was a twenty-four-hour operation, the resulting difference of me treating everyone according to the golden rule was $1.5 million in increased productivity per day.

Right then and there is when I cultivated my core tenant: "It doesn't cost a penny to be kind." Although it's not traditionally considered part of a work ethic, being kind and respectful is the first step in my own. Not only does it help you function by keeping your spirits in a positive place, but it encourages your team to work harder, to focus, and to do their best. Don't get me wrong. There were still times I had to create a paper trail to deal with a problem employee, but because of my reputation as someone from management that was good to people, I was supported in taking the necessary actions in the rare instances they were required. The simple, ethical choice to respect my team members and to treat them like people rather than production assets outperformed any management school motivation tool by far.

"What caused me to reboot my career was a series of moments in time where I asked myself, 'Is this how I want my life to be? Am I happy doing this? What are the things that energize me and bring me joy?'"

—Lakecia

YOUR WORK ETHIC WON'T
BEAT THEIR BOTTOM LINE

I started my career forecasting the cellular market in the early 2000s. At that time, we were looking to Asia to see the emerging trends of color displays and integrated cameras in phones. My first exposure to a corporate vice president and his team came when I was twenty-five years old and forecasting demand for products for the next three years. It was the holiday season, and I was in a closed-door meeting with the heads of finance, supply chain, and marketing. We were briefing the leader on the outlook for the business (which we refreshed quarterly) to make investment decisions and to update the outlook for the shareholders and the board of directors. It was one of my first times with a bird's-eye view of how the levers of the business were pulled and how fast some decisions are made (and how little data they are based on).

One of the scenarios we ran that session was how closing a factory would affect the division's balance sheet. The depreciation for the factory was a large drain on the business unit's books. This factory was less than three years old and employed three thousand people in the local community. On the week of Christmas, we were considering closing it, even though it was making a profit. Growing up in the shadow of the automotive industry, I was likely more sensitive to the topic. I had seen what happens to a community's quality of life when large manufacturing employers pull out of town, and this discussion hit me hard. When I was going through engineering school, I never imagined putting my analytic skills to use to justify a decision I so strongly disagreed with from an ethical lens. Although the factory was a drain on my specific group's profit and loss statement, it was a net positive for the overall company. I grew up a lot in the following couple of years and lost my naive belief that, if you work hard and stay positive, you will automatically succeed in your career.

At the time, I was beginning to feel like my life was following a pattern of missing out: I'd gotten a job at General Motors the year *after* they stopped providing pensions and had joined Intel right before the dot-com bust; I watched the value of my stock options drop by 75 percent when they vested four years later. I was frustrated. I had worked my way up the corporate ladder quickly, but I also had a nagging suspicion that my ladder was leaned up against the wrong building. I left a very good boss at a company I loved because burnout from traveling one hundred thousand miles a year was taking its toll. Quitting was the only way I could think of to regain my humanity.

In the end, I realized that my own work ethic would never beat the company's bottom line. My priorities wouldn't—and couldn't—shift the company toward what I saw as the best way forward. Trying to turn a for-profit company's focus to accomplish a not-for-profit's mission is like swimming against the

> "I rebooted my career out of pure frustration of having to 1) work for someone else, I wanted to be my own boss 2) watch subpar customer service ruin my clients' lives, and 3) an inner conviction that I was created for so much more than selling payroll and that I was 'playing it safe' and wasting my God-given talents."
>
> **—Mary**

current. It will eventually wear you down. In order to do that, you either have to find a company whose mission aligns with your own work ethic before you arrive or create the culture yourself by starting your own company.

WHAT DOES WORK ETHIC TEACH US?

Much of my work ethic was nurtured as an athlete growing up, and it has provided crucial lessons throughout my life. I started figure skating at the age of three, and I grew up in ice rinks. Some of the lessons I learned on the ice have served me well in corporate America without compromising my boundaries.

- You fall ninety-nine times before you stick the landing on a new skill, so get up and try again.

- Learning how to fall and get back up without injury is essential; relax into it, and don't fight the momentum.

- Judging is a subjective mix of precision and artistry; sometimes it doesn't feel fair.

- When you stick a landing, you feel like you are flying and truly free; it was worth all the blisters and bruises it took to get there.

These lessons served me well in the first phase of my career, when I was learning how to be an individual contributor, and they helped me to end on the right side of the sink-or-swim culture of tech. But before I got there, I had a year that forced me to draw on all of those ice-skating lessons I'd learned and put them to work.

"I'll never forget a mentor saying 'Just because I'm good at something doesn't mean I have to do it forever.' It struck me like lightening. I learned that it's okay to be bad at something before you're good at it. In fact, it's a requirement of entrepreneurship. I can figure things out."

—Allison M.

2017 started with a toast to the best year yet. My passion project—using AI to fight online child sexual abuse—was just fully funded by Intel and was announced on a global stage at Open Summit. I was promoted to lead the initiative and was given a team to showcase the power of artificial intelligence (AI) for societal good. Little did I know that it would prove to be the toughest year I have ever faced.

In just a short time, it seemed like everything hit at once. I sustained a debilitating back injury, my boss quit, and then my job was eliminated six weeks after I hurt myself. I also started noticing signs of secondary trauma from the victim stories I had been exposed to through my advocacy work. I couldn't sleep, I was having intrusive thoughts, and I couldn't stop thinking negatively about the world. Unfortunately, without good wellness practices, this is all too common in social justice work.

Although I had moved into a new job at my company, I still had the responsibilities of my old job to complete. With a demanding day job, a passion project, and two kids under the age of six, my self-care was nonexistent. I had a hard time balancing the prioritization of my own pain with trying to prevent the suffering of children.

After testing revealed that I had a herniated a disc in my

lower back and that the material was sitting on my sciatic nerve, I knew I was not in for a quick recovery. My doctors kept using the term "severe injury" once my MRI came back, and I did not sleep without morphine for months. It would be about a year before I was able to comfortably walk again. Lacking healthy boundaries, I was prepping my SXSW panel while attached to a morphine drip in the hospital. Then I travelled to Austin by myself when I could not walk around my own block.

Pushing my body like this took a toll on my recovery, my family, and my well-being. By the end of the year, the funding for my project had dried up. And while I was seen as a traditionally successful director of a tech company, it was far out of alignment with my own definition of success. I felt like I was surviving but far from thriving.

I spent months wrestling with the conflict between what I was raised to believe success should be (job security, title, salary) and what lifted my energy (mission, impact, social good). By 2018, my husband had seen me spin my wheels long enough and gave me the nudge I needed to go out and launch a startup.

The amazing people I had collaborated with on my passion project across the tech industry were there to help every step of the way. It felt as if the universe was rising to meet me on this important mission. From funding to talent to partnerships, things kept falling into place for my company, Minor Guard, to be born.

> **I felt like I was surviving but far from thriving.**

For the first six months of Minor Guard, everything was running smoothly. Then, my technical cofounder was offered an opportunity to return to Apple that was hard to refuse. His career change was a point to reflect on and evaluate my own core values. What was more important to me: impacting a billion lives or making a billion dollars?

After some deep self-reflection, I knew I had to focus on impact. It is a core value of mine. We mutually agreed he could advance our vision of safer platforms for children better from inside a huge international company than by trying to wield influence from outside, in our little startup. We knew we needed additional resources to continue, so we brought in another cofounder and started to explore the competitive landscape for potential collaborators. I took our technology roadmap for the Android market into Bark Technologies. Bark monitors texts, email, YouTube, and more than thirty apps and social media platforms for signs of issues like cyberbullying, sexual content, online predators, depression, suicidal ideation, threats of violence, and more. As of 2021, Bark was a leader in content monitoring for children and was used in over 3,300 school districts. Just like Bark, which gives parents early warning signs that a child needs help, I would like to help you recognize your burnout signs sooner and make the leap to a more sustainable and fulfilling mission-based career.

It may seem simple, but the lesson here is profound. Working harder doesn't always mean success. In order to reach my goal of making an impact on children's lives, I couldn't just power through work and life and meaning and parenting and everything else. Those straws very nearly broke this camel's back.

Instead, I had to focus on what I truly wanted and abandon the parts of my work life that didn't fit within that purpose. "Success" defined by other people doesn't actually mean anything if it isn't what you need or want. By learning to say no, I was able not just to balance but to align my work and life. Instead of just working hard, I learned to work toward something important.

NAVIGATING FORWARD

- As a leader, the key to unlocking people's innate work ethic is treating everyone with dignity and respect.
- A company won't align with you. If you need something beyond what your current organization can provide, find a new one that provides it—even if you have to create it yourself.
- Working for a purpose will always take less out of you than working for a paycheck.

CAREER REBOOT ACTION:
BUILD COMMUNITY

Work challenges can be overwhelming. Find different ways to connect, learn, and share with others outside the office. Join a book club, volunteer, or connect with a religious community group.

CHAPTER 2

Vicarious Trauma

The notice came in on a Friday in March: "School is not safe for children. We will pivot to distance learning starting on Monday."

I did not panic but instead went into cruise director mode. Okay, I didn't plan on having the kids home for the next week or two, but we can make it fun. With both my husband and I working from home, we could share parenting and teaching duties in addition to our sales jobs. I printed the charts for activity schedules for school-age kids, ordered lots of air-dry clay and other crafts, and set out to create some structure so that I could get at least half a day of work in during normal business hours. When I was tucking my seven-year-old son into bed that Sunday night, he looked me in the eye and said, "Mommy, my dream has come true!"

I replied, "What is that, honey?"

He said, "I get you to teach me every day for school."

And I realized his dream was my nightmare.

I really respect and admire teachers and their seemingly endless patient, caring, and giving nature. At the same time, I have never been told "You know what you would be great at? Elementary school teacher!" But now I found myself homeschooling a second grader and a third grader for the next three months. The first week or so was fun, and we had some awesome quality time together, but that didn't last.

I remember a day where my daughter was supposed to do a flipchart video reading a five-minute passage to her teacher. My daughter was struggling with reading at the time, and what the teacher thought would be a fifteen-minute activity was stretching out to two hours with many breaks, crying, pump-up speeches from mom, and even a dance party to try to push past anxiety and fear and finish the assignment.

Once the assignment was finished and submitted, I got a message from the teacher indicating that my daughter "seemed sad" in the video. The teacher wanted to make sure everything was okay at home.

I wanted to scream, "We are all sad" after losing hours of our lives to this.

I felt ashamed that I could not make learning fun for my child. By the end of the school year, it was clear something had to give. We were all restless, burned out, and frustrated. But my children would not return to a brick-and-mortar school for fourteen months, and my husband and I would not have a break from round-the-clock work and childcare until the kids' grandparents were vaccinated twelve months later.

Today, schools are back open and vaccines are widely available, so it is tempting to go back to business as usual. But, for marginalized groups in the workplace, that is simply not tenable. The flexibility required of working parents before 2020 was different—that was an hour, scheduled weeks in advance, to take a child to the orthodontist or attend a once-a-semester parent conference. Now, it's take over teaching and daytime care for a week—starting tomorrow morning—while the school is closed again. Working parents today may need to shift to caregiving on a moment's notice, and they have to be able to respond without fear or shame. The weakness in the social infrastructure that supports working parents has been exposed, and employers who want to retain top talent will need to fill the gap.

In November of 2022, according to the Bureau of Labor and Statistics, the number of people missing work due to childcare problems exceeded one hundred thousand for the first time.[1] This is greater than the number of parents missing work during the height of the pandemic, likely due to the simultaneous surge in COVID-19, the flu, and RSV in 2022.

My point is: The old business routine doesn't work anymore for some or even most people. The cookie-cutter approach—everyone in a company living in the same area, sitting in a car potentially for several hours every day to drive to an office—doesn't work for most people anymore. Companies would have better employees and less turnover with more flexibility now. But your own health is certainly better off if your work situation reflects your life needs.

This radical flexibility is facilitated by technology innovation, but there are also many dangers to mental health of constant virtual connection. Our children are also now threatened in their schools—from bullies, exploitative adults, and even gunmen. It's crucial that we are all aware of these additional stressors for today's parents and that we balance addressing them with the rest of our lives and work.

> "I knew my previous status wasn't sustainable. I wanted to be the best parent, spouse, and professional, and it was my responsibility to figure out how to make that feasible. I had to recalibrate my priorities. I wanted to give my own children the depth of attention and engagement I had been giving to my child clients. My kids deserve(d) that."
>
> **—Heather**

DIGITAL SAVVY AND SAFE TEENS AND TWEENS

During the lockdown, many young people turned toward technology to stay connected to their friends and restore some sense of normalcy to their lives. With school being fully virtual, being on devices for hours on end became normalized. And with most sports and extracurriculars on hold, there was not much of an alternative for peer connection. We now know that this has had a significant impact on the mental health of a generation. The problem is, Pandora's box has been opened. Even schools rely more heavily on ubiquitous technology. We can't shove the genie of screen time and being constantly online back in the bottle overnight. There are strategies for maintaining a healthy balance, but no one size fits all; you'll need to find what works best for your family.

When the pandemic hit, needless to say all my rules about screens went out the window by month two. I tried to hold the line for online gaming, but by the next school year, my kids were feeling more and more isolated not being able to play with their friends. I eventually gave in, first on *Roblox*, then on *Fortnight*. Even experts on online safety are human, and I can only manage so much.

My empathy for what the kids had already gone through outweighed my concern from pediatricians that "most kids meet their first stranger in online game rooms; that is where the worst threats from pedophiles start." We practiced our online safety drills on what to do when they are exposed to something that makes them feel uncomfortable, we set up parent controls on their accounts, and we have had them play in common spaces in our home ever since. Isn't it interesting that we all grew up with safety drills in schools, but schools don't prepare our kids for what do when someone crosses a boundary with them online? I have never had to use my tornado drill training, but I guarantee that every child will have some kind of unsolicited inappropriate content sent to them while online before they turn eighteen.

In 2017, my company, Minor Guard, conducted focus groups with teens and tweens across the country and learned that many girls don't make it through junior high without being asked for a naked photo from their peers. Human traffickers prey on this "new normal." Provided on the next page is a sampling of what we heard from kids across the country who you wouldn't consider high-risk.

This behavior the teens experienced is unacceptable, period. But it also normalizes this awful behavior, making it hard

"I think about what I wear. I don't go anywhere unescorted. I don't date because boys scare me, and I'm falling behind in my online school, which is reducing my potential to fulfill my dream of being a doctor." (age sixteen)

—

"I received my first dick pic from a boy at school at age thirteen on my Kindle." (age fourteen)

—

"You don't make it through the first week of your freshman year of high school without one of your peers sending you a naked photo." (age sixteen)

—

"I turned down admission to my dream school to opt for community college because after being sextorted at fourteen, I wasn't convinced I could stay safe on a big campus." (age seventeen)

"It's becoming harder for girls to distinguish what is pornography because of celebrities, and they are copying it."

—Pediatrician

"Sexting is the new first base."

—School administrator

"This behavior spans all socioeconomic levels."

—Church leader

for kids to recognize when adults are crossing boundaries or grooming them. Pedophiles are also taking advantage of the Internet's anonymity to infiltrate online friend groups. This is not the threat we expect from *Unsolved Mysteries* or the nightly news; the threat isn't from some stranger in a van but from the screen in your child's own room down the hall. There is a big difference between adolescent curiosity and coordinated criminal behavior of adults to groom children for human trafficking or child sexual abuse imagery.

We also interviewed pediatricians, school administrators, and church leaders to get a better understanding of what they are seeing on the front lines for tweens today. What we learned from our focus groups is that, across the United States, the adults in our children's daily lives are in denial about the risks their children face online:

What many don't appreciate is a statistic that John Shehan, vice president of the Exploited Children Division of the National Center for Missing and Exploited Children shares: "Forty percent of child pornography reported to law enforcement are generated by children themselves."[2]

It's the split second that a kid decides to make a seemingly innocent decision to send a nude photo to someone they trust but who they shouldn't. We are expecting kids to have the judgement of adults, while predators are weaponizing their phones against them. It's not a fair fight. It can set off a chain of events, including felony charges for creating and distributing child pornography, sextortion, or being registered as a sex offender for life from a small bad decision.

To help educate more guardians of tweens and teens about their roles as a gatekeeper for the digital lives of young people, here are my top five tips about what to say to a child when they are given access to the digital world:

- It is my device, not yours: Write up a contract on how each device is to be used that you both agree to.

- Teach your kids that they should never expect anything to be private on their phones or online. Bark Technologies provides a free technology contract template that parents may find helpful.

- Tell them, "I am not concerned about the choices you will make online. I am concerned about the access I give to others to make bad choices that affect you."

- Remind them that, if they come to you, you will not panic and take their device away. You are here to support them. Secrets can only live in the dark, and they need you alongside them for teachable moments online just like in analog life.

- Teach your kids technology emergency drills: When they feel uncomfortable with something they see, experience, or do online, teach them to *stop*, *walk*, and *talk*: Stop what they are doing, walk away from their device, and talk to a trusted adult.

No decisions you have made about apps, usage, and privacy up to today need to be final. As the wise Maya Angelou says, "When you know better, you do better." Phones are not diaries, and children should not expect for you to be hands-off with their device until they are eighteen. It gives them an excuse to set boundaries with their friends on what they are sent by putting the blame on you. It also gives them a safe space to process what they learn about the adult world with a trusted adult. If parents are not able to provide context for challenges, a stranger on the Internet is more than willing to step in.

So what does this all mean for working parents? When we were growing up, kids were at school, and problems that happened during school were handled at school. Today, in a 24/7 digitally connected world, schools cannot know what's going on, and it falls to parents to be engaged whenever needed. That need often surfaces during working hours. There are some affordable mistakes that can wait. But there are some digital challenges that are life altering—suicidal ideation or sextortion, for example—and you, as the adult, the parent, need to have the flexibility to address them immediately.

> "My children needed me to be braver than I was; I needed make a change in my career."
>
> —Deanna

FROM ALOHA TO TRAUMA

In 2015, I was selling laptops to education institutions and got to see how the public sector worked as a system. We were in an elementary school in Hawaii during a sales call when the principal received an emergency alert from law enforcement to go into a lockdown due to an armed gunman on campus. For three hours, we sat in the dark, waiting for the shooter to get to our area of the building. I remember seeing teachers exuding calm for the children; meanwhile, I was in a conference room in the fetal position, panicking and writing goodbye letters to my family. That experience changed my perspective on the resources and compensation for this traditionally female-dominated field.

While in the lockdown, I saw a stream of teachers leading their classes to the designated area for these types of emergencies. They were the ones on the front lines keeping the kids calm by singing, hugging, and nurturing with their leadership. It dawned on me for the first time that these teachers should be receiving hazard pay similar to many first responders. They were the ones in the line of danger, with little to no training and at the mercy of policies decided by administrators who were often not present when these emergencies arise. By the grace of God, the shooter that day did not make it past the parking lot, but we did not know that for the hours we spent cowering in the dark.

Three months later, it was time for me to send my oldest child to kindergarten, which I did not realize at the time was going to be a post-traumatic stress disorder trigger for me. On the second week of school, my sweet five-year-old came home and shared how they practiced hiding under desks in case "bad dogs or bad people" came into the classrooms. Being a technology insider, I knew there were many software solutions on the market that could assist schools in early detection of issues. The ability to engage intervention early can often help to avoid a crisis before it happens.

Seventy-five percent of school shootings are discussed in private channels on social media up to two weeks before the event. It was not the lack of a signal we are dealing with, but the ability to detect the moments that matter and that are going to go from talk to a credible threat to something that will spread trauma for the rest of people's lives.

As I brought this information to my public school's administration, I was met with strong resistance from the administration on monitoring the technology tools they were providing my children for threats of violence, suicidal ideation, and bullying. I spent two years trying to get the district to adopt free and commercially available software that could do just that. In a unionized system, where the district administrators are often trying to maintain the status quo, I was not able to make any progress toward protecting any of the thousands of children in the district. The school superintendent said, "I already don't have enough councilors to deal with the problems I know about. Why would I want to know about more?" No progress was ever made.

School systems, which are traditionally staffed by women, are not being funded for basic needs and supplies, are not offering a livable wage, and do not meet minimum safety requirements we expect out of most work environments. I don't think this is an accident. It is an outcome of not valuing the invisible labor that is traditionally supported in society by women. Working for years inside that system to change it wore me down emotionally and physically. I finally moved my children to a public charter school that used school safety monitoring technology already. It was not the outcome I had hoped for, but working against a system that was allergic to innovation made it impossible to make progress for the well-being and safety of the public school's staff and students. We must not wait for our school to be in the news to take a more proactive approach to protecting our students and teachers.

"I was in a senior leadership position for the world's largest organization and had asked for the ability to work from home, just one day a week. I was told no. They said they needed my energy at work. I realized I was working at a place where I wasn't heard. Each and every one of us deserves to have our needs met, at work and at home. If they're not getting met, it's time to make a change."

—Amy

In order to stay on top of the evolving threat landscape for children, parents need the space and time to be present for moments that matter when their children are exposed to toxic content, relationships, or environments, including cyberbullying, sextortion, human trafficking, suicidal ideation, and school shootings. Children are resilient, but there is no replacement for the role of trusted adults in their lives when moments of crisis happen. We can't outsource processing the complex world we live in to technology, and these issues can arise anytime in a 24/7, always-connected world. Giving parents the space to address issues as they arise without shame will allow situations to be put in perspective and long-term damage to be minimized.

We need to start treating employees like the adults they are and to give them the space to navigate when and how they accomplish their work in order to accommodate the demands on them outside of the office. If we focus more on the business impact and results, and less on perceptions and politics in the office to measure someone's annual performance, we are well on our way to create a better workplace for everyone.

NAVIGATING FORWARD

- Demands on today's working parents have increased as their children enter the "always on" connected world. Working parents need the flexibility to parent when needed and be trusted to manage their time.

- You have to operate technology in certain environments, or they will not perform as advertised; the same goes with humans. If you are starting to feel glitchy, it may be time for a reboot.

- The school itself is now a potential source of danger. Make sure your children—and their school's leadership—are prepared.

CAREER REBOOT ACTION: START AN ENERGY LOG

It only takes five minutes a day to create a data log of your energy fluctuations. Write down how your energy level changes throughout the day. Be sure to notice what activities and interactions drain you and which energize you. This distinction is crucial to creating a life with more of what builds you up.

CHAPTER 3

We All Need
Self-Care

Living in the twenty-first century can be anxiety provoking. I don't remember the terms *safe spaces*, *trigger warning*, and *trauma* being part of the lexicon when I was growing up. Rates of alcoholism, domestic violence, divorces, and PTSD have all climbed during the COVID-19 pandemic. With society opening back up, it is back on parents' plates to worry about safety risks for their children from every side, not to mention the parents' own struggles.

I have adopted good tools for wellness from my days working in content moderation for online safety. Secondary trauma is a hazard of the job, and with my PTSD diagnosis from working alongside law enforcement to track down pedophiles, I spent five months with professional counselors learning how to better take care of myself and to set and hold clear boundaries. In 2020, those tools became very useful as we lived through a global pandemic and experienced a collective trauma together. The more trauma triggers people are exposed to, the more people will need to care for their mental health proactively. We have all heard the training on airplanes: "In case of an emergency, put on your own oxygen mask first before helping others." These are wise words when you are on the ground as well.

Modern employers need to recognize their role in providing trauma-informed training to managers in order for them to accurately identify and coach people who may be reacting to a trigger while in the workplace. Many employers have resources available to employees for support, but they are buried in benefits packages and not used at a high rate. The stigma of mental health issues prevents many people from feeling safe to take a medical leave or to talk to a mental health professional. The simple act of giving more resources and training to frontline managers on how to navigate this emerging leadership skill can increase retention and engagement from their most valuable assets: their people.

This is a new area of training that companies are still wrestling with. Some of the most innovative companies are developing bespoke curricula to address this emerging leadership capability. Don't wait for attrition issues before investing in training of this kind for your managers.

"I know I have to fill my cup before I can fill anyone else's."
—Lakecia

THE MYTH OF WORK–LIFE BALANCE

"Burnout occurs because we are trying to
solve the same problem over and over."
—**Susan Scott**

Before the pandemic, people described me as a force of nature
and an executive who could juggle most anything you threw at
her. Burnout was an amorphous idea, something that happened
to other people who could not "gut it out" at challenging times
and show up for the moments that really matter as a leader—or
so I thought.

It was not uncommon for me to be leading a company,
keynote speaking, and serving on boards of directors, all while
volunteering at my kids' elementary school and in the community. As women of a certain generation, we have been raised with
the myth of work–life balance, that modern women could have
it all if we were just better at managing our time, demonstrating
our worth in a meritocracy system, and advocating for ourselves.

My experience with this myth in my own career began with
denial: I worked as if I were immune to burning out. But when
the responsibilities of my rapid career advancement collided
head-on with the needs of my growing family life, I felt my
"strength" of being able to work through anything was actually
a weakness.

Twenty years into my career, I found myself on the verge of a
burnout, both mental and physical, that I had convinced myself
I would never experience. I would get defensive or frustrated
in meetings if anyone questioned agenda items I thought were
done or if they asked me to add more tasks to my to-do list. In
a highly matrixed organization, I found myself managing the

expectations of numerous stakeholders who had no visibility into the extent of work on my plate. Often, instead of setting a boundary, I just did the extra work.

As I got more and more exhausted, I found myself being shorter with people I cared about, becoming frustrated by minor inconveniences, and daydreaming of being left alone. It seemed like the idealized version of womanhood that was painted in my youth by the first generation of women's rights leaders was miles away from the societal support required to make it feasible. Caretaking responsibilities were meant to be a team sport, but in American culture, they are handled more like a solo sport much of the time. If you were able to achieve in the workplace, it was important to keep this labor invisible and to look like you weren't breaking a sweat.

Working women are taking on the brunt of the emotional labor both at home and in the workplace. Humans are designed to effectively handle stress in small doses, but not indefinitely. A 2022 article from McKinsey suggests that distress, depression, and anxiety are widespread in the working world. Approximately a quarter of their respondents reported signs of burnout.[1]

The myth of work–life balance being the key to success was strongly ingrained in us. And our national culture of working

> "Start by making time for rest or a hobby, something that doesn't have to do with work. Giving your brain the space to do something else brings great epiphanies that help your approach to work."
>
> **—Emily**

until we burn out, which is highly cultivated in modern work-places, is leading to a disturbing trend of employee retention issues. The term *quiet quitting* has become popular since the pandemic to describe employees no longer willing to use discretionary energy outside of the scope of their job functions.

According to an interview with Amelia Nagoski for the *Atlantic*, "Quiet quitting . . . is not actually quitting. Instead, the quitter keeps their job and chooses to do only the bare minimum rather than go above and beyond." A Gallup poll showed that perhaps more than half the working population in America fit the definition of quiet quitting.[2]

An example of quiet quitting is Amy, a successful marketing executive with three young children. With an MBA from the University of Chicago and decades of digital marketing expertise, she is in high demand as a consultant. She was able to balance the needs of her clients on her time during the shutdown by hiring nannies to care for the kids while she carved out time to do her billable work. What she did not see coming was a midpandemic divorce that added selling the house, counseling for the kids, court dates, and moving to her plate. She compensated by meeting the commitments for her clients per their contracts but not going above her hours or providing strategic guidance on how to advance long-term brand goals as she usually does. She is showing up every day and doing what she has committed to, but her brand of going above and beyond is not her primary focus right now. All of these life-changing events have had a cumulative impact on her over the years. She dreams of a day when her must-do list is something that can be accomplished in a twenty-four-hour day, but with school interruptions, illnesses, court dates, and the toll of moving adding up, she is focused on getting her annual contracts renewed and not dropping any balls that would affect her custody during a contentious divorce.

High-performing members of your team may be quiet quitting or on the path to leaving. If you can remodel your own career to one with balance, you empower your employees to do the same. You will earn their loyalty and discretionary energy to accomplish the vision and mission you have set out on together. People have to see it to be it.

In order to grow where you are, there is an element of surrender involved. When you let your fear of not meeting expectations go, you can edit the role you are in to amplify your unique value and continue to grow your impact. Along the way, you may need support for your mental health, and there should be no shame in seeking out professional advice.

Take my client Paul, for example. With a degree in astrophysics from UC Berkeley and a PhD from Harvard, he is a published author, startup founder, thought leader, and father of four boys. A fifty-six-year-old man who had been an innovator his whole life, Paul went from being a breadwinner with a stay-at-home wife to a single dad overnight. When he unexpectedly became a widow, he had to sustain his career without the partner he had had since the age of eighteen to keep things running at home and pay for two kids in college and two more to follow in the next couple of years. His income exceeds $500,000 a year, but the stress to keep all the balls in the air is taking a toll.

Paul began suffering from high blood pressure and panic attacks. With the future bills piling up, he did not feel empowered to quit his job until he could find a suitable replacement. I urged him to take a three-month medical leave to stabilize, dream, and plan.

In the first month, he returned to daily walks with his dog and playing music together with his boys in a family band. The time together was restorative for all of them as they deeply mourned their loss. In month two, he reached out to his network to learn about interesting areas of innovation in healthcare and startups. By month three, he had replaced his full-time job with an equal salary, working with one of the world's best medical research hospitals and as a chief strategy officer for a promising healthcare startup company. His hours were back to manageable, his blood pressure returned to normal without medication, and he got engaged to be married. His hobbies now include music, woodworking, and traveling with his new wife.

All of us need time, space, and support to address our health. Our mental, physical, and emotional health are also intertwined, as we saw with Paul. In order to stay healthy, you must create that buffer for yourself, and a career reboot may be just what you need.

NAVIGATING FORWARD

- Your strengths can become your weaknesses when they are overused. A strong work ethic is a good thing when taken into balance with your humanity, but can cause burnout fast when left unchecked.

- Demands on today's working parents have increased as their children enter the always-on connected world. Working parents need the flexibility to parent when needed and should be trusted to manage their time.

- Workplaces need to reduce stigma on mental health issues and support employees as they address the needs of their families during this time of increased challenges.

- If we look at the lack of societal supports for mid- and senior-career working women, it is no surprise we are seeing a rise of quiet quitting. It is the only labor that they *can* quit when they are burnt out.

CAREER REBOOT ACTION: RECHARGE

Plan activities to distract or recharge yourself. Taking a break allows our brains to relax and let go of thoughts or messaging that are not serving us or helping us solve the problem in front of us. Scheduling downtime or shifting our thinking can open up new lines of thinking and bring new ideas to the surface to help us in our work.

CHAPTER 4

Post-Traumatic Wisdom

> "If I were to summarize in one sentence the single most important principle I have learned in the field of interpersonal relations, it would be this: Seek first to understand, then to be understood."
>
> **—Stephen R. Covey**

COVID-19 has created a whole new class of cognitively and physically disabled workers. While the full health complications of COVID are yet to be seen, there are two big challenges that we are already aware of. The first is that some people do not seem to recover and are diagnosed with long COVID. The second is that the last few years have taken all the stress and trauma that society was already reckoning with and put it on steroids.

The Centers for Disease Control and Prevention, in a study that examined nearly two million patient records, found that

"I was sitting in a conference room at work, while my furious boss is screaming at me for something I or my team did or didn't do. In my head I was wondering, 'Once I get out of here, can I catch the head nurse at my mom's facility before her shift is over?'"

—JeanAnn

one in five COVID survivors ages eighteen to sixty-four and one in four ages sixty-five and older developed a health problem that could be related to long COVID.[1] If the findings prove accurate for the broader population, millions of people in the US alone may have some form of the condition.

The National Institutes of Health (NIH) was interviewed by CNBC about their own long COVID study. According to Dr. Stuart Katz, one of the NIH study's coordinators, "Long COVID can impair a person's ability to work, which could have economic consequences for their families. The severity and duration of patients' long COVID symptoms vary widely. The population of people permanently disabled by long COVID is likely a fraction of those who have some form of the condition. Still, there's likely a very large number of people who have a disability from long COVID."[2]

Dr. David Putrino, a physiotherapist and director of rehabilitation innovation at the Mount Sinai Health System, in New York City, was also interviewed by CNBC about long COVID. According to CNBC, Dr. Putrino said, "Many patients who come to Mount Sinai for treatment suffer cognitive impairments that are similar to traumatic brain injuries, commonly referred to as *brain fog*, in which they struggle with speech fluency and making plans to deal with life's daily challenges. They can also often have abnormal heartbeat, tingling sensations, painful cramps, and feelings of anxiety. Any form of physical or mental exertion worsens these symptoms. As a consequence, about 60 percent of the long COVID patients at Mount Sinai struggle to continue at their jobs." The CNBC article also quoted Dr. Putrino as saying, "They either had to shift to part-time work from full time, retire early, or became unemployed. Almost all the patients report a deterioration in their quality of life due to their symptoms."[3]

Here are my realities of living with long COVID:

When I run out of energy, it affects me both emotionally and physically. I start high at the beginning of the day, and I am drained sometime before bed. On stressful days, that can be noon; on calm days, it can be 6:00 p.m. I don't have a way to predict until I am almost on empty.

When I am struggling, it is hard to ask for help. I don't have the energy to explain why I need the help. Unsolicited suggestions are frustrating and embarrassing. I have been managing this for years and the same things don't work from one day to the next.

What I think I can do in the morning often is not accessible to me by the time it is time to do it. Because I don't want to disappoint or explain to people, I often push though. That makes me feel worse for the next day by living beyond my energy budget.

I can't behave well enough to not have flares and remissions. It is not going to be fixed with mindset, diet, and exercise. It can be better managed with pacing strategies and acceptance of my body's signals.

I am slowly losing all the ways I play to enjoy myself (dancing, skating, skiing, hiking). I am willing to pay the price of recharging my joy when I have the energy because I don't know until the moment I go if I can. I am scared that, the sicker I get, the more isolated I will become. It is my worst fear.

Some days, I feel great and forget I am sick. Such days are becoming fewer and farther between. I want to enjoy them when I can and not focus on what is to come. Often, people with very good intentions misunderstand the severity of my pain. I feel judged and like an annoyance when this happens. It happens daily. It is more painful when it comes from my loved ones.

I was raised to believe I can do anything I put my mind to. That is no longer true, and it makes me sad. As an athlete, I was accustomed to performing through pain, and I know how to do it. I have learned over the past few years that this behavior now ends with me in the ER or in bed, unable to work. I try hard to find the balance, but it is constantly shifting.

EVOLVING HEALTH BENEFITS

Our systems are going to need to evolve to meet the needs of millions of people like me who are newly disabled or have increased health burdens. We will need to educate and provide reasonable accommodations for people who are new to needing these supports and advocacy. This often requires self-advocacy and boundary setting, which can be uncomfortable, so I am sharing some of the boundaries I put in place over 2021. Long COVID forced me to learn about my new energy budget, and I'd like to provide people with the framework that I had to establish since I was early in needing accommodations in the workplace.

Some accommodations available for the workplace may include medical leave from employment. In America, you can drop down to thirty-two hours per week and maintain health-care benefits; anything below that, and you lose your insurance. They will put you on COBRA for your healthcare benefits if you drop below that threshold, which can be very expensive. You can also set time limits on how and when you work for your employer. For the first year of my disability, I worked no more than twenty hours per week and no more than four hours per day on Zoom calls. This allowed me to lay down and rest as my pain escalated during the day. You may not get the boundaries right on the first try. Continue to talk to your doctor, and continue to evolve them as your recovery progresses.

You can apply for short-term or long-term disability if you can no longer work full time. To qualify for long-term social security disability, including Medicare, don't quit without documentation that you are disabled.

You should also consider hiring a patient advocate. Healthcare systems are not set up to help patients manage the number of appointments and specialists required to deal with complex chronic health issues like long COVID. I currently see ten specialists a month, and they are not coordinated or aligned with each other. It is mentally draining to educate and advocate for yourself with so many people when you have chronic fatigue to begin with! If you qualify for Medicaid or Medicare, you can request an ombudsman from your state to do this service for you free of charge.

"Genuine listening can change lives. Each and every interaction we have throughout the day gives us the opportunity to provide someone with the most cherished gift of being heard. We don't need to agree, we don't need to offer advice, but we can listen, and then follow up to show them they've been heard."

—Amy

One of the greatest challenges I've faced and that many people with long COVID face is people not believing that the symptoms we suffer are real. When in doubt, believe someone as a reliable witness to their own pain. It is hard enough to function in a body suffering with long COVID. Not being supported at the workplace, home, or with friends can deepen the sense of hopelessness for those already suffering.

NAVIGATING FORWARD

- Employers will need to evolve the workplace to accommodate a new class of ADA-protected employees affected by long COVID or needing mental healthcare following the past years of trauma and stress.

- Determining the accommodation needs for a recently disabled worker will take time as many conditions have flares and remissions. The employee will need support to work with their doctor until the correct balance can be struck.

CAREER REBOOT ACTION:
ESTABLISH ROUTINES FOR SELF-CARE

Eat, sleep, and exercise are crucial. Schedule all three into your daily calendar. Have structure throughout the day: Get up at the same time, have your meals at the same time, go to bed at the same time. Getting into a rhythm with your days can help to create muscle memory for positive habits that support self-care. Self-care is critical to building resilience.

CHAPTER 5

#MeToo; Now What?

During the early years, when I was first building my career, I rarely found my gender to be a challenge. In fact, since I worked in technical sales, I always viewed my outlier status as an advantage. It was not until I returned from having my second child that I experienced what it felt like to go from the in-group to the out-group.

The day I returned from my second maternity leave, I was informed that my position selling engineering solutions had been eliminated during my absence. They consolidated my position into a colleague's role. They also made it clear that, if I made it a problem, they would be happy to have my husband removed as a vendor for the company. I had a new role selling electrical components, which was one I would not have chosen. In the blink of an eye, I had been relegated to an entry-level role fifteen years into my career. I'd been ranked within the top 5 percent of the company in performance during my last review

"I got the worst performance review of my life from my manager while I was in Corporate America. I just had returned from maternity leave and honestly believed that I was delivering my best work. I was incredibly proud of myself for juggling being a first-time mom and a working mom, only to receive devastating news that I was performing below expected levels. This blow came out of nowhere without any warning signs. I came home that evening, feeling dejected, beaten, and wondering what the heck I was doing with my life."

—Visa

"I went out on maternity with my twins and got the call two weeks later that a male peer of mine was being promoted to become my manager. I asked why I was not asked to interview for the job and they said, 'You have kids now and clearly don't want it.' I said, 'Actually, I do, and I should be allowed to interview for it.' I ended up having multiple interviews up the chain and got the management job."

—Hilary

"I couldn't get any flexibility from my employer even though I was having breast health issues from pumping after coming back from maternity leave. The mother's room was so far from my desk that I had to use extra time outside breaks just to keep from getting mastitis (even then, I didn't avoid that health issue altogether). I ended up with thrush on my nipples as well because I didn't have adequate time to clean my pump parts. They would not allow work from home at the time, which would have solved all these issues and allowed me to grow with the company."

—Deanna

cycle before I'd gone on maternity leave. During my next review cycle, I was told that it was my "husband's job" to pay the mortgage and that my money was "for shoes." That was the justification given for why I shouldn't care about being switched from a six-figure guaranteed income to a commission-only pay structure. Needless to say, I wasn't convinced.

Later that first week back, I went on my first customer-facing calls, hours away from my home. I planned the day to include breaks to be able to pump and figured it would be hard but doable. I carpooled with a coworker so that we could share the driving. I set up some meetings for us at a water-bottling plant and a lumber manufacturer. During the first meeting, the plant manager slid me his phone in the middle of my colleague's presentation and said under his breath, "Do people ever tell you that you look like her?" It was a topless photo of a porn star.

I had spent my whole morning crying, having to leave my baby, and with two children under the age of three at home, the last thing I was thinking about was my sexuality. My colleague tried to be supportive but came off creepy. He said, "You really bounced back well from having a baby; you are going to get a lot of attention from men because of that. Guys *really* like that." It was only years later that I learned the most popular search term on pornography sites after *teen* is *MILF*.

After that incident, Jeff, the colleague who took over my pre-maternity job responsibility, and I were meeting for mentoring to help me get back to my original position in the organization. He started commenting about how beautiful I was. Eventually, he propositioned me to join him on a fictitious work trip to San

"In a meeting in another country with a customer, I was the only female in the meeting and later at dinner. The local account manager who owned the customer relationship and made all the logistical arrangements for the trip asked if he could show me a picture of his family and I said that I would love to see it. He showed me his phone and on it is a porn picture of two naked women kissing and touching and both women resemble my hair color, age, and complexion. I was appalled and felt very unsafe. I tried to ignore it and avoided him the entire night. I didn't speak to him again. That night I worried about how I was going to get to my hotel safely because now I did not feel safe riding with him alone. Rather than focusing on building a positive business relationship and closing the deal with the customer I was worried about my safety in a foreign country."

—Kristin

"I learned from a coworker that some of the senior software developers I worked with called me 'boobs.' I asked who, and only learned one name. I asked a trusted manager what to do; he said you do what you feel comfortable with—reporting it to HR, approaching him, both. I decided to approach him first; he denied it. Then I took it to HR. And that was really uncomfortable because HR asked, 'Do you want to file a formal complaint? If you do, he'll be fired.' It seemed like so much responsibility on me. I liked him personally, we got along, I didn't want him fired over what he said, but I did want him held accountable. I decided not to go forward with the formal complaint. I did tell him I didn't appreciate it and he said he'd be more respectful. He eventually did get fired (not because of me)."

—Allison G.

Francisco, where he could "show me a good time." My husband "would not have to know." I declined.

It was clear that this environment, which had been nurturing, supportive, and a great place to work for the five years before I had children, where I was a top performer, had shifted. It was time to put on my own oxygen mask and get out. It took me a year to create my exit path, and I stayed at this employer during that time in order to maintain my medical benefits for the kids. But leaving was the only option and was my top priority.

When I saw a trusted HR partner at a meeting, I pulled her aside and shared my story without disclosing the names of my harassers. I had one foot out the door; I was in the final round of interviews to return to tech in a new job at a different company. But I knew that I was not the first person to experience sexual harassment in the office or to be demoted for being pregnant. I thought I was helping the women I was leaving behind. Boy was that naive.

During my last week in the office, I was called into a conference room by HR and a "witness." I was asked to tell the full story of the affair I was having with my direct manager. I immediately replied that I never said that and that I was offended to have the accusation documented.

They asked, "So you recant your statement?"

I replied, "You can't recant something you never said."

It went back and forth like this for over fifteen minutes before we moved on. I was so relieved to get out of that room and put all of it behind me. Little did I know, that was not going to be allowed.

When I reported sexual harassment at work from a colleague,

"I entered a room for a presentation to a senior leader and my manager at the time looked at me and asked, 'What have you got for me to fondle?' He wanted the copy of the spreadsheet I was carrying in my hand. As a woman with curves, I was shocked. I stood there unable to move or react. Another manager in the room jumped in. He immediately encouraged my manager to 'walk the comment back.' My manager doubled down and said he didn't feel what he said was inappropriate. As his request started to penetrate my shocked brain, I dropped my papers on the table and walked down the hall to the office of the manager of my manager. I interrupted his phone call and let him know that if I was still working for my manager the next day, there would be legal consequences. This was the last straw for me. My manager had been harassing me in other ways for months. The next morning, I came in and found I was no longer reporting to my manager. I found out later he was sent for training to help him understand what harassment was and how to recognize language that was inappropriate in the workplace. He did try to apologize with an 'I am sorry you felt harassed.'"

—Vikki

"Through most of my career I experienced some sort of harassment in every role. As a young professional I didn't know what was 'normal.' I was also afraid that my job would be in jeopardy if I said anything. Recently I had a situation with a client and I did not hesitate going to their manager. They called to apologize and said, 'I'm sorry YOU took what I said wrong.' I asked if this was an apology. He said yes. I asked him to try again, this time without blaming me for his behavior."

—Teresa

I experienced retaliation, and my reputation was slandered broadly. Years later, I would still have strangers mock me in public about "being the one who sued the company"—which never happened. I only reported my experience after accepting a new job elsewhere, in order to advocate for the women left behind. I was not the first person to get demoted for being pregnant there, nor the first to endure blatant sexual harassment from customers and colleagues. I am sure I was also not the last, but the best I could do at the time was to put my own oxygen mask on and get out of that toxicity. I am still recovering from watching my career go down the drain when I was at my most vulnerable and from experiencing what happens to victims of harassment when they speak up for themselves.

After consulting multiple lawyers, it became clear that if I pursued legal action, the most I would get was the equivalent to a year's salary before the fees, time, and energy to go through litigation. I also learned that 99 percent of women who move forward on this path never work in their chosen field again. No way did a single year's salary become an acceptable payoff for losing the right to work as an engineer from a top tier school with fifteen years of experience. Ultimately, I chose to leave, but the sting of victimization followed me for many years, as it does for many women. I am not saying this doesn't happen to men, but it does not happen nearly as often.

I later learned that the person harassing me was having an affair with another employee in the department, even though he was married with children. He cast a wide net looking for vulnerable people. He continued to be promoted and has not faced any consequences I am aware of to this day.

"I worked for a male-dominated company in a male-dominated industry. I was twenty-five and the only female on my team. The Regional Sales Vice President, who had been with the organization for over twenty years, walked up to my boss and me after an important presentation and the first thing he said was, 'Who did you sleep with to get this job? Next time, wear a skirt.' I was shocked, humiliated, and immobilized. My boss looked at me, then looked at the SVP and said, 'Perfect example of what NOT to say in the workplace.' It was laughed off. My boss asked me if I was okay after that, and I said yes. That was a lie, but I didn't know how I felt. Whenever I had to be around that individual, I felt incredibly uncomfortable. Ten years after that event, I had to sit next to him at dinner. He introduced himself like it was the first time he had met me. He wasn't inappropriate at dinner, but I had lost respect for him and many of the leaders he surrounded himself with. I left the organization shortly after that dinner."

—Amy

"I loaded trucks for a shipping company while I was in college. The women's bathroom was on the far side of a very large distribution facility so it was a bit of a hike to get there. One day, a man leaned out from a station I passed and tried to grab my breast. He was moaning and touching his crotch with his other hand. I was quick and avoided the free hand and ran to the bathroom. I gathered myself and went to HR. They did an 'investigation' and told me that the man had developmental problems and that I should wear longer shorts (they were already almost knee length) or long pants. In the summer, the trailers could reach 125 degrees inside so wearing long pants did not seem like a reasonable solution. I quit shortly after."

—Deanna

My experiences were before the #MeToo movement. I must admit I thought this problem was isolated at my workplace; it was very eye opening a few years later to see how widespread the issue was and how accepted this level of toxic behavior was. Around 38 percent of women have experienced sexual harassment in the workplace, and 75 percent of sexual harassment cases in the workplace are unreported.[1]

Forced arbitration clauses and nondisclosure agreements, which apply to 55 percent of working women, are meant to obscure our understanding of how prevalent discrimination and harassment are in the modern workplace. I am grateful for people like Gretchen Carlson, who advocated for the 2022 #MeToo bill that "ends the use of forced arbitration clauses specifically for sexual harassment and sexual assault claims." The bill allows victims of harassment to bring the dispute to court. It also applies retroactively to previous cases.[2] President Joe Biden described the problem like this:

> When it comes to sexual harassment and assault, forced arbitration shielded perpetrators, silenced survivors, enabled employers to sweep episodes of sexual assault harassment under the rug, and it kept survivors from knowing if others have experienced the same thing in the same workplace, at the hands of the same person.[3]

When I experienced harassment in 2013, I felt very isolated, and that isolation made me think this was a unique, personal problem. I attributed it to working in the construction industry, even though I had also experienced it in the automotive, technology, and restaurant industries. It was the first time I felt silenced. At times, I even felt erased, and by people, including women, I'd cared about and considered friends. I was forced out of one social group that cost me an important relationship with a mentor, all because the woman who led the group didn't have the facts and believed falsehoods that my standing up for myself might cause problems for the company and the people that worked there.

Additionally, the aftermath of this harassment was so impactful to me because of the threat of it affecting not only my career but my husband's. I did not mind standing up and advocating for myself, but I did not feel comfortable putting my husband's career on the line as well. I was not going to throw away my career, my husband's revenue, and my children's healthcare, so I changed my environment.

I would like to report that from there I experienced no further sexual harassment. I would be lying to you if I said that was the case. The tragic part was that, when it happened on a customer trip, my instinct was to hide it from a very supportive and well-respected manager. I was doing well, and I did not want to be perceived as a troublemaker. I found reasons to miss a meeting where I would have to be on calls with my harasser. I am sorry to all the other women he harassed.

I had to go to counseling to break my habit of defusing this type of behavior with humor. I would freeze when someone violated my boundaries or superficially laugh it off, instead of speaking up. Kasia Urbaniak said, "It's that moment when you're on the spot, or in a position to stop something, change something, set a boundary, say no, claim credit, or even offer your own brilliant insight on the situation . . . yet absolutely *cannot*. It's the moment you are frozen on the outside, but on the inside, fractured language, feelings, assessments are whirling around a racing heartbeat inside a body that doesn't move and a mouth that just won't make words."[4] I learned to avoid the freeze from Urbaniak's TEDx talk "One Simple Trick to Reclaim Your Power." I had to learn to reply with something appropriate in the moment instead of coming up with the perfect comeback forty-eight hours later.

I learned from working with a therapist that practicing a simple prepared response to situations like this in the mirror is key to being able to feel empowered to navigate the unexpected. I had to prepare to address issues early, as they arise, and to expect people to test my boundaries.

It is never comfortable to be put in this kind of position, but when you can direct the attention back to the person who is being inappropriate, it hands the problem back to them. They will be the ones left holding the hot potato of shame. Everyone has their own methods for defusing uncomfortable situations. I usually defaulted to minimization and humor, but if we want to transform the workplace for inclusion, we need to take back our power. We need to make sure predators don't feel empowered to hunt at the office. Take courage from the fact that, since I started addressing these incidents head on and not avoiding them, the amount of times I have had to deal with them has reduced. One uncomfortable five-minute conversation with someone who may not know they have crossed a line beats months of your discomfort being in the room with them when things have escalated. And for those who jump gleefully across the line, you can let them know that you are not a victim and will not let them act this way. If the culture of the team you are working in doesn't support your standing up against harassment, it may be time to find another place to contribute your talents.

I used to be a rock and roll DJ. My last radio gig was broadcasting to twenty million listeners a day for XM Satellite Radio. Alas, radio is a major boys' club. I felt squashed, invalidated. And, of course, there was sexual harassment GALORE:

- sex jokes, locker-room talk, 'compliments'
- porn playing on people's laptops
- my boss asking me if when people heard my voice 'did they get hard?'
- my boss asking me if my "hands were clean" so that I could hold his penis while he urinated
- a fellow DJ asking me for birthday spankings in an email
- another fellow DJ offering to do me favors only if I would trade him blow jobs
- an investor putting his hand on my leg
- another investor insisting that I go on a "date" with him for my birthday where he hit on me profusely
- another investor insisting that I get a man to raise money for the company because I clearly couldn't do it on my own
- another investor telling me that I wasn't cut out to be a CEO because I had no experience (he was trying to diminish my ability so he could then lowball the price of our company and purchase it out from under us)
- another investor telling me how much I was like his younger daughter, inferring that I was a child/naive

- another investor showing me cartoon pictures of a penis-designed drinking apparatus that he was marketing
- all manner of investors 'mansplaining' me with patronizing, unsolicited advice.

I'm tough. It just washes off my shoulder. The only time it really makes me mad is when people are in my way, hindering my work, then I'm frustrated.

To some degree, it's comical. Because you can't believe it's really happening, over and over again. I have never ever been comfortable reporting it. HR, in every instance I've ever experienced in every job, has always been a nightmare, never my friend and always on the side of the company. Any exchanges I ever had with HR they literally told me I was imagining it and that I was lying.

I was in an uber-hostile work environment that triggered PTSD and my body started to manifest the stress physically. I can no longer type at all without excruciating pain through my fingers, arms, hands, and elbows, and I have to use voice activated software. I can't even touch my phone without a stylus without extreme pain. Eventually, it became so bad that I was diagnosed with a partial permanent disability. So, I moved to another music-related company, but it was the same thing all over again. I was miserable. Always crying. It was such a toxic situation because I hated my job, I was in an overwhelming amount of pain and felt stuck.

No one gave me any accommodations. HR again accused me of lying. Everyone thought I was making up the pain.

—Kate

NAVIGATING FORWARD

- Although retaliation for reporting harassment in the workplace is illegal, it is not uncommon.

- Forced arbitration clauses and nondisclosure agreements apply to 55 percent of working women, which obscures our understanding of how prevalent discrimination and harassment are in the modern workplace.

- Prepare to address issues early, as they arise, and expect people to test your boundaries. Document these moments in case you need to involve others.

CAREER REBOOT ACTION: RESTORE JOY AND SELF-ESTEEM

Do something that brings you joy. Play guitar, restore your car, do some woodworking, take up glassblowing, go to the movies, go to the park, hike, bike, run, draw, paint, read, write. Take the time to reconnect with or discover new, nonwork related activities. Embrace your talents to help bolster your self-esteem. Relaxing your brain and giving yourself time to shift gears often brings solutions to the problems you may be facing in your work.

CHAPTER 6

InteGRITy

"For years, I've noticed that the universe speaks to us in whispers. If we ignore the whispers, we get pebbles of warnings. If we still don't pay attention, we get bricks of problems, and if we're really hardheaded, eventually, the entire brick wall comes crashing down."

—attributed to Oprah Winfrey

Grit is my way of functioning in the world. When I get overwhelmed or overworked, it can become my greatest liability. This strength turns into a weakness when it is overused; I sometimes take on a sense of responsibility for issues that are not feasible to solve in a single lifetime. Midcareer, I sometimes feel like a hermit crab who has outgrown their shell. I am sprinting across the beach toward a bigger shell, hoping not to get picked off by a seagull en route.

I had to learn to temper my sense of responsibility and to set healthy boundaries between my home and work life in order to regain control of my natural inclination to be a

> "I felt I needed to be more present in MY LIFE. My work has always been so all-consuming that I rarely had time for introspection. Once I actually took that time, however, I felt it in every fiber of my being and I couldn't turn back from what I discovered: it was time to reboot my career and redesign my life."
>
> **—Tiana**

workaholic. When I saw my greatest strength—my powerful grit—being turned into a weakness, it shocked me into learning to pace myself. A career is a marathon, not just a sprint to the next promotion.

I was raised in the generation that was told, "As long as you focus on work–life balance, you can have it all." Then that was updated to "You can have it all, just not all at once." During the "great breakup," I think many other working moms are quitting the only responsibility they can—their careers. The social structures required to support them—paid parental leave, quality childcare, and not being "mommy tracked" when returning to work—are still issues America is grappling with in 2022.

When I returned to tech in my midthirties, I had more commitments outside of work, with a husband and young children. It forced me to optimize every moment of my day, like I was on a treadmill that I could not stop from the moment I woke up until the time my head returned to the pillow at night. It also happened to coincide with potty training my two-year-old son. Since I was on back-to-back conference calls for eight or nine hours most days, I got used to ignoring my body's signals of fatigue, hunger, and even needing the bathroom. Four months after returning to Intel, I was at the doctor's office for holding my pee too many times and giving myself an infection. It was a humbling lesson that I needed to prioritize my basic human needs over the demands of any role. It was a pebble I ignored.

Overapplying grit to achieve someone else's goals for you is not sustainable or recommended. Every yes you say to the world is a no you say to yourself and your family. Choose wisely.

THE CONSEQUENCES OF MISALIGNMENT

In 2016, my body started sending consistent signals that I was overdoing it. At first, it was subtle, and I was still able to reset over a long weekend. But there were many times I pushed myself too hard to meet a deadline for work or a need for my family, and I was no longer bouncing back in the same way.

My first brick, as Oprah might say, came on a Tuesday. Getting out of my car while lifting my laptop was enough to get me admitted to the hospital for three days. This is when I herniated a disc in my back, and was at the beginning of what would become a yearlong healing journey to walk again. I would be lying if I said my body had not been sending me warning signs to slow down for a couple years before this incident, but all of my time as an athlete had trained me to push through pain to ultimately attain my goal. The only problem with that strategy was that, in my midcareer, there was always a new ring to reach for and no endpoint or trophy in sight. It took not being able to walk without opioids for nine months for me to learn that overcommitting in all areas of my life would cost me dearly in the end.

"I was not happy. I let unhappiness build up in me. I let trivial things bother me. I don't think I was always nice or the person I wanted to be. It was not healthy. I was not healthy."

—Teresa

Now I've learned my lesson, and I watch myself for the first signs of trouble. The way I know I am on the fast track to the wrong place is when I start to get short with people. First, it's anyone who asks me to redo something or take on more work. My impatience escalates until I feel like I should call someone after a meeting and apologize for interrupting. That's when I know I am misaligned.

For you, misalignment may show up in a different way—a dry mouth, a queasy stomach, or a blinding headache—but we all have ways that our body processes stress and tries to send us signals when we have done too much for too long. No one will ever have a career that does not include some aspect of work that drains their energy, but when it gets to be more than 25 percent of the time you spend in your life, it can start to have an impact well beyond yourself. The challenge is that, in this day and age, it is hard to slow down enough to even notice when you are not functioning in alignment with your values, including your health. If you are a working parent, it can be even more pronounced, because you are switching between jobs all day and well into the night.

Ultimately, the key to finding long-lasting connection, contribution, and contentment is to align your personal values with your work and home life. It may sound naive to think that you can make money doing what you feel uniquely called to do, but I can guarantee you, from my lived experience, that when you apply your strongest talents to a mission-inspired goal that benefits society, a company, or a community, you can find a way to turn it into a career. Since shifting my focus from success to significance, I have increased my salary while reducing my hours, and the impact of my work in the past five years is greater than the cumulative work I did the first fifteen of my career. This was not what I expected, but I have five years of data to support this even during one the most disruptive societal events in the past hundred years.

> **The key is to align your personal values with your work and home life.**

FINDING MY MISSION

When I began working in online trust and safety for technology in 2015, there were approximately twenty people with jobs that were aligned with my personal mission—to apply innovation to improving the lives of marginalized women and children globally. Today, artificial intelligence ethics and digital safety is a defined industry across governments and the private sector. In 2017, my ethics were challenged by a decision that a business partner made, which impacted my project. As a result, I decided to move from a traditionally successful corporate career to entrepreneurship.

I started my career as an engineer forecasting the cellular market supply chain in the early 2000s. At the time, we talked about how phones might one day have color displays and cameras, but at no point did I envision the phones of today being used to weaponize children against themselves. But that's exactly what is happening, right this minute, for the purposes of human trafficking and child sexual exploitation. In 2016, while working for Intel, I attended a meeting in Washington, DC, where I had a chance to speak with the CEO of the National Center for Missing and Exploited Children (NCMEC), John Clark. He said, "Handing your child a smartphone is like dropping them off in the most dangerous city in the world and walking away."

That one meeting literally changed the course of my career and my life. As a parent, it shook me to my core. Many don't know about the NCMEC, although most are probably aware of their work. They produce country-wide Amber Alerts and are the mandatory reporting location for all child sexual abuse material identified by Internet service providers, law enforcement, and the public.

In late 2017, I was at a crossroads. During the time I'd been at Intel, we had set out and accomplished our mission of accelerating the coordinated national response of reports of child sexual abuse material from thirty days to twenty-four hours from technology companies to law enforcement. The number of reports to be processed had grown from five hundred thousand in 2013 to eight million by 2017, and their team of twenty-five analysts could not keep up with the volume doubling every year, so we used a combination of automation, artificial intelligence, and computing upgrades to better equip them. We also helped the NCMEC move to cloud computing, updated their data center to deal with the increasing volume of video content they needed to process, optimized their software to run more efficiently, and refreshed their cybersecurity process.

Even though we had accomplished our stated goals, I wanted to do *more* to prevent the creation of this illegal content in the first place. As we dove deeper into the data, I learned the surprising fact mentioned in chapter 2: More than 40 percent of child sexual abuse material is generated by children themselves! This happens when a child decides to take and send a nude photo to someone they mistakenly trust. A chain of events is set off by one decision. If technology had the ability to stop kids from being able to take these photos in the first place, we could've prevented twenty-six million traumatizing instances of child sexual abuse material from circulating in 2020. It would free up law enforcement resources to take down prolific offenders who are grooming and extorting hundreds of children over their lives. I was committed to this goal.

But by 2018, the company I worked for was under new leadership, and I no longer had the executive sponsorship I needed to continue the work. We had committed over four million dollars in resources to accomplishing this goal, but I knew there was still much more work to do. I realized I could not go back to the traditional measures of success I had relied on to guide my decisions in the past: career advancement, money, and power. None of those things would bring me what I needed.

I would redefine my career to focus on significance. I would infuse more meaning into it.

As a working mom of young children, the expectations from the corporate world were out of alignment with my responsibilities at home, and I was on the edge of burnout. When you are burned out, you will reach the point of diminishing returns with work much faster than if you are proactive about your wellness.

Over coffee with one of my mentors, Gregg Descheemaeker, I shared my idea to leverage advancements in artificial intelligence to block a child from being able to save an explicit image they took on their phone. When I was done, I asked him to talk me out of doing it.

He replied with a question that helped get me out of my own way: "If I go to your funeral, and it turns out you never tried to do this thing, even though it would likely fail, would you be okay with that?"

I had never felt clearer on my answer: *No*. I recognized that as a technology insider, trust and safety expert, and sales professional, I was uniquely qualified to lead this initiative. This was not a technology problem, but a will-to-act issue. I knew how to align innovation with influential leaders across the industry to make impactful change. Without Gregg, I would not have taken the leap into entrepreneurship. The next step was to find a strong, technical cofounder with a complementary skill set, not someone who mirrored my strengths and my blind spots. Mahmudul Hasan was that complementary cofounder for me. After that conversation with Gregg, Mahmudul and I finally left our global tech jobs and launched our company, Minor Guard.

Not only did Gregg inspire us to pursue our dream, but he also provided the seed-round investment for Minor Guard and later served on its board of directors.

At Minor Guard, my work finally fell into alignment with my values. Our mission was to make kids safer, both online and in real life. Today, our technology roadmap can be seen in Chromebooks from Lenovo and on the iPhone 12+. When we started our company, it took more than 130 choices to block your child from saving a naked photo of themselves on their device. Today, with a family iOS account, it can be accomplished by adjusting one single setting. That success did not come easily, nor did it come without long working hours. But I was able to regain my balance during this season of life by taking charge of my work life and protecting my time.

This meant letting go of certain corporate responsibilities that kept me in back-to-back meetings for most of the day, often bleeding into nights and weekends as I worked to support a global team. Instead of accepting increasingly blurring boundaries, I refocused my time and attention on leading: setting the tone for the company's culture, establishing our cadence, and defining and reviewing our key performance indicators.

Since we aimed for an acquisition of Minor Guard within eighteen to twenty-four months, we needed to stay laser focused on our priorities: building our intellectual property, innovating for product–market fit, and prioritizing making tech safer for children.

It is crucial to leverage your mission to build a team of supporters who can help to accelerate your minimum viable product and amplify your reach with beta customers. We made sure we had people who were invested in our company's journey on our board of directors or advisory board, as well as workers throughout the company who were committed to the mission. Working with the team I had curated, each member of which was equally passionate about our mission, made the days fly by. My shift to entrepreneurship had taken me from focusing much of my time on politics and alignment within a large corporate structure to removing roadblocks for brilliant people to apply their skills to a higher cause. This shift allowed me to focus on my recovery and energized my creativity to meet the moments that matter as a leader.

The year 2018 was not only the most rewarding of my career, but it also accelerated my growth as a leader. That year, I broadened my business acumen, built my brand, and executed on my commitments to investors. Since I had a team to support me, I was able to prioritize my health and accelerate my impact on the technology ecosystem. But addressing misalignment isn't a one-and-done experience. It's an ongoing practice of mindfulness and attunement to the ebb and flow of your stress and satisfaction levels. As your career grows and changes, so will your needs and priorities. If you ever have the feeling that your work life has become unsustainable, believe yourself. I have never met a woman who said, "I ignored my gut instincts, and everything turned out great!"

In 2018, my partner and I exited Minor Guard. My career transformed once again, but this time, I had clarity about my personal mission: I would focus on making a significant impact. I now serve as a board member and advisor for technology-forward startups in a variety of industries, including healthcare,

> "I love the life I am living today. My health has improved because of it. I wake up everyday feeling connected and fulfilled. It was worth the scary journey to get there."
>
> **—Visa**

supply chain, human resources, and digital safety. I find that I love working directly with operators to accelerate their vision of success and help them drive revenue. As a consultant, I work with some of the largest technology and healthcare companies on their digital safety strategies for data. My team often brings together the public and private sectors to address issues like human trafficking, Federal Drug Administration approvals for artificial intelligence used on clinical medical devices, and reducing toxicity online. Now, I specialize in helping executives make the invisible visible and help them find the actionable wisdom in an ocean of data to derisk companies in cybersecurity, digital safety, and privacy.

As a natural product of my growth as a person and a professional, the consequences of misalignment are a lesson that I have had to relearn from time to time. But each time I find myself succumbing to stress, I notice the signs and make a conscious choice to focus my energy on bouncing back and making better decisions moving forward, instead of criticizing myself for repeating an error. Be kind to yourself if it feels like you're becoming your own worst enemy at times. It's hard to break out of old behavior patterns when you've relied on them in the past—even if you know now that they aren't serving you—and a little compassion for yourself will go a long way.

> "It's an old lesson that fear and excitement are two sides of the same coin. When you're excited for something new, it overwhelms your fear of the unknown, and you can make a change."
>
> **—Vikki**

NAVIGATING FORWARD

- The key to finding long-lasting connection, contribution, and contentment is to align your personal values with your work and home life.

- Stay focused on your work mission, keep your priorities straight, and protect your time and energy. Is your role to facilitate daily Zoom meetings or to remove roadblocks for your team?

- If you have a feeling your work life has become unsustainable, believe yourself. I have never met a woman who said, "I ignored my gut instincts, and everything turned out great!"

- Authenticity matters. If you are spending more than 30 percent of your energy trying to fit into a predefined box, it only leaves you 70 percent of your talent to stand out as a leader!

CAREER REBOOT ACTION: INCORPORATE WELLNESS PRACTICES THAT FIT YOU

Start slowly, and integrate more wellness practices into your life. A few you can try include these:

- Go outside for a morning walk to help clear your mind before starting the day.

- Tether exercise to an activity you enjoy, like watching a favorite TV show while walking on a treadmill.

- Charge devices in the kitchen and not in the bedroom. Check in with yourself before you check in with the online world each day.

- Try ten minutes a day of meditation. There are many apps available to provide a guided meditation experience.

PART 2

Employer
Headwinds—
The Future of Work

CHAPTER 7

How Work Has Changed for Women

I t is easy to see the pain and suffering around us and to be consumed by the despair and injustice of it all. But in the larger context, we can see that gravity keeps us from drifting off into space and our hearts beat without our will to do so. I have a severe allergy to injustice for women and children. When I witness it, my body instantly rejects it. It makes me agitated, frustrated, restless, and angry.

As women age, we are subjected to so many systems that are set up with a patriarchal structure that it is sometimes hard to discern where the discomfort originates. Is it the ubiquitous shame triggers for women that tell us our acceptable behavior is on a tightrope of opposing values? Be assertive but not aggressive, or you will be labeled a bitch. Be a good girl and follow the rules, which only benefit those in power and are meant to

> "While many companies have leadership training for women, it often has little impact as the promotional decisions are based on who you know and being part of the 'in' crowd (the 'good old boys' network)."
>
> —Sadie

keep you in your place. Motherhood layers on additional social responsibility to manage the social lives of the family, including at school, sports, social events, and religion. These all require delicate behavior management in order for you to be accepted by the group. And these groups are mostly run by men.

Many women find that even when we use superhuman will to do the impossible year in and year out, the more we succeed outside the home, the less likable we are to other people. This phenomenon is known as the *competence–likability dilemma* for women leaders: Women, unlike men, are rarely perceived to be both competent and likable. The sad truth is that most of us don't find strong, competent women easy to like.

In 2003, Francis J. Flynn, at Columbia Business School, conducted an experiment. He took a case study about Heidi Roizen, a successful female venture capitalist and changed the name to Howard Roizen. Everything else about the case study remained the same. He gave half of his class the Heidi Roizen version and the other half the Howard Roizen version. He asked the students to rate how competent and how likable Heidi and Howard were. Both female and male students found Heidi and Howard to be equally competent, but the students tended not to like Heidi. They thought that she was a little too aggressive and out for herself. Neither female nor male students wanted to work for or hire Heidi, but they all thought Howard would make a great colleague.[1]

In our society, women are penalized when we behave in ways that violate gender norms. Our gender stereotypes show that women should be kind, nurturing, helpful, supportive, and deferential; while men are traditionally expected to be decisive, competent, assertive, and strong. So the dilemma for women is that the qualities we value in leadership, such as assertiveness and decisiveness, go against the societal norms of what it is to be a likable woman.

But in the end, it doesn't really matter what other people think of you. Whether you are considered likable or not for being competent, you should be celebrated for doing your job well. If your company's culture or leadership disagrees, it may be time to find a new one.

TWO GENERATIONS OF WOMEN AT WORK

My mother was a professional student until I was ten. She first pursued a master's degree in social work, and then got another in business administration from the University of Michigan. This was no small feat; the first time she took the GMAT, she scored in the bottom 5 percent. Instead of taking this as a sign that she should stick to social services, she used it as motivation to study. A year later, she scored in the top 5 percent.

She then entered graduate school with a few disadvantages. The first was that she had not taken the college level business and math courses that most of her peers had. The second was

"In general I was overlooked or bucketed in a category of not 'leading the right way.' That meant not being loud and more forceful with my decisions and arguments. Not pushing the team to deadlines the same way my peers did (which I thought was overly micromanaging). I felt that workplace generally failed at times to see the different way I led was a strength—it was much more team-oriented than individualistic. And the workplace was promoting individuals."

—**Allison G.**

that she had an elementary-aged child to care for in addition to school and a husband who worked night shifts. When she graduated, we took a family vacation to celebrate her four years of hard work and her new career at the National Bank of Detroit as a commercial loan officer.

As a young child, I remember thinking that my mother looked quite silly in her business suits and bowties, but at that time, I did not appreciate how ridiculous it really was. A suit was the dress code for her job, but in the 1980s, they did not sell them off the rack in the women's section of the store. She had to get them custom made so that she could look like "one of the guys." For the next twenty years, I saw my mother try to fit in with the finance crowd. She would come home crying to my father about how she never felt like she could be successful there. I remember being puzzled about why my father's work life as an engineer seemed so relaxed while my mother's seemed so stressful. In hindsight, it makes a lot more sense.

Women are often expected to go above and beyond what men do, even today. We are expected to constantly perform at work while also doing most of the emotional labor at home. We are expected to embrace the behavior of our male colleagues, even when they are less talented or efficient at the job and to take whatever behavior they throw our way, from microaggressions to outright aggression.

When my daughter was in second grade, I was the volunteer who came in monthly to do STEM (science, technology, engineering, and math) education enrichment activities. Each month, I would plan a project-based learning activity, go buy all the items for the kids to build something they could take home, and explain the skills they learned by doing this fun project together. It would take, on average, eight hours of prep time once I factored in the research, shopping, instruction time, and everything else. I did this project every month of the school year except for one.

One time, I asked my husband to bring in a thermal camera that he sells for work to show the kids. His prep time was approximately twenty minutes in all, due to the years he has spent perfecting this training, since we had the camera in our garage and it is his job to do demonstrations with it. When he arrived at the school, there was a marked excitement from both the students and the staff that was lacking when I had showed up alone. Before he left, the teacher asked for him to pause so that the vice principle could come to personally thank him for such an amazing opportunity for the kids. I will acknowledge he did a great job that day, and it was awesome for him to inspire the kids. But I have not experienced a tenth of the fanfare for spending an hour of my time volunteering. Four years later, my kids still talk about this visit and how cool their friends and teachers thought it was when their dad came to school with a thermal camera.

The expectations for men are not just lower than those for women. They are often nonexistent. If a man makes even a marginal effort, it is often praised and appreciated far beyond what his female counterpart would receive, and this happens in every other aspect of American culture, especially at work. But it doesn't have to be that way. Many modern companies are intentionally creating cultures of equity and inclusion (look for those terms in their job ads!). Many woman-owned businesses may also be more understanding of the daily lives of their employees. In the end, if you can't find a culture to fit what you want from your work life, you can build your own.

FORGING FREEDOM

Katie is a client of mine who had been climbing the corporate ladder for nineteen years at a large global management consulting firm. She was viewed as a rising star and had a very good reputation as a senior director for customer delivery.

She was also the person who got stuck buying all the raffle prizes for the customer golf tournaments. She organized the "Day of the Woman" event for the company. She was also a single mom of elementary-school-age children and the primary breadwinner for the family. Most days, her day job took up at least ten hours, and she was juggling between family help, nannies, cleaners, and Amazon orders to make sure that all the people in the house were well taken care of and no balls were dropped. She was exhausted going into the pandemic, and then the schools closed for fourteen months. In the middle of all this, she got remarried and moved, and her family

"After being on a team for ten years, I asked my boss to ask if I could apply for a role that opened that was my dream job. He agreed the job was perfect for me, but I was the top producer and the only one willing to travel globally for extended projects, and he asked me to give him four to five more years. I didn't know what to say. I asked if I could still apply and he responded that I could, but I wouldn't get his endorsement. He had been with the organization for thirty-four years and was one of the most respected men in our organization. My option was to go around him, knowing I would burn a bridge with a man who helped me get to this point and likely lose my current job. I feared retaliation. I didn't apply. I then left after seventeen dedicated years with the organization."

—Amy

relocated to a new area. At this point, her natural talents (grit, determination, and resilience) were putting her on the fast track to burnout.

Meeting with her financial advisor for guidance on blending finances with her new husband, Katie had an epiphany from a simple question: "What are your hobbies?" Her husband quickly answered: running and travel. Katie, on the other hand, went blank.

What working mother has time for hobbies? she thought. She was surviving but far from thriving. She yearned for the feelings she had earlier in her life as an equestrian; time in the saddle made her feel truly free. With the demands on her plate, there was simply no room for more.

Katie decided to make a change, to find a way to build that

freedom into her life. She was able to find a similar role with the same salary at another company, leveraging her skills and experience but with more manageable hours. She is now settled into married life, she doesn't work beyond forty hours a week, and with the kids getting back into school, she has time to reinvigorate her passions. She now spends three days a week at the barn with her daughter, who she discovered has a matching passion for horses. They have quality time riding together and participating in horse shows. She no longer struggles to know what her hobbies are or what she is passionate about.

THE GREAT BREAKUP

Many women are looking for a new way forward. We want to contribute, to work hard and for a meaningful purpose. But we also want to live our lives. A McKinsey and Co. 2022 Women in the Workplace report found that women are "demanding more from work, and they're leaving their companies in unprecedented numbers to get it. Women leaders are switching jobs at the highest rates we've ever seen—and at higher rates than men."[2]

This study cites three main reasons for the trend:

- Women leaders want to advance, but they face stronger headwinds than men.

- Women leaders are overworked and underrecognized.

- Women leaders are seeking a different culture of work.

Women face professional headwinds, such as networking outside of the office in environments where women are not as commonly welcomed. It is harder to find mentorship and sponsorship without first forming a true connection. This is harder in an office environment. Many marginalized groups connect with others in the workplace via employee affinity groups, but most of these groups are run on the unpaid labor of the very employees who they are meant to serve, which adds to their burnout and doesn't get recognized or rewarded at review time. Many leaders are no longer willing to trade hours for pay without consideration for the company's ethics. They want to see leadership behaviors at all levels aligned with the aspirational diversity, inclusion, and sustainability commitments made by the company's board and C-suite in mission statements and annual reports.

I like to focus on the things you can control. If you find yourself facing hurdles your male counterparts do not, you may need to shift your career based on the organization's mindset and limiting beliefs. It is also possible that you are operating in a system that is patriarchal in nature and that the only change left to make is to move on. Find an environment where the leadership is less biased and where the culture truly incorporates inclusion as a lived value. Use this time to explore if there are other environments where your efforts, talents, and skills can take you farther, faster.

My job out of college was in supply chain planning. It involved huge spreadsheets, detail orientation, and tons of math. I was able to force myself to sit down and do the work, but it took significantly more energy for me to do that than it did to face customers in a sales role, which was much more aligned to my interests and talents. My success was tethered to reclaiming my discretionary energy from doing things I was not good at, and it took me a long time to focus on my strengths. That is an example of a mindset shift fixing the issue.

But that may not be enough. You may need a workplace or even career shift. Take some time to determine exactly what you want, then go out there and get it. I call this a *career reboot*, and it can reset your professional outlook just like a juice cleanse can reset your body.

NAVIGATING FORWARD

- To be human is to be biased. Check if you are holding your female and male employees to different standards.

- Women experience a phenomenon called the credibility–likability dilemma. At a certain point, you may be in a position where what makes you great also makes others uncomfortable. That is okay; it is their issue to manage, not yours.

- Emotional labor is still labor. If you are spending half of your energy on fitting in, it only leaves half for your creativity and contributions.

- You can't behave well enough to be treated with respect if that respect is not available to women in your current corporate culture. When you sense that the environment is toxic, start making plans to find another place to shine.

- Many of society's rules were established to set and maintain a traditional power structure. If you are not included in that power structure, it does not serve you to observe rules that don't violate laws.

CAREER REBOOT ACTION: NETWORK

Reach out to someone you admire or who always leaves you with a positive impression. Ask for thirty minutes of their time to better understand their approach and how they arrived at it. How do they set boundaries—and stick to them—to remain focused on their mission? Do they use certain tools to recover when life gets out of hand?

CHAPTER 8

Innovation, Impact, and Inclusion

Many decades and dollars have been spent trying to increase the representation of women in STEM careers, with mixed results. We see a large increase in the number of women graduating from college with degrees that qualify them for jobs. The challenge is that, as they move through their career leadership journey, we see sharp drop-offs in the number of women represented in management and even more sharply in the C-suite and on boards of directors. Many slowly leak out of the pipeline for leadership as the wear and tear of being in an environment still unaccommodating—and unwelcoming—to women, particularly during the midcareer window when leaders are selected. If we focus on the long game and leverage flexible options for supporting women during these prime caregiving

"My manager created a new leadership position on their staff and filled it immediately without allowing me or anyone to apply or interview for it. Then they moved me and my entire organization to report into the new leader. It created an awkward situation. I tried to make the best out of it because I really liked my job and the people I was leading were such an amazing group of people doing incredibly important work for the company. Reality was I was being squeezed out. It should have been clear to me then that my leadership was no longer valued, but it took months and some other awful things to happen for me to realize the significance of that moment."

—Kristin

years, we can accelerate innovation, inclusion, and impact for the workplace and our human legacy.

In July of 2021 the Gates Foundation released data to show just how detrimental the COVID-19 pandemic had been to women's equality around the world. Even as the economy started to recover, the Gates Foundation reported that two million more women were expected to leave the workforce that year, adding to the thirteen million who left in 2020. This mass exit is largely due to job loss and caregiving responsibilities that disproportionately fall on women.

"The recession and the early trends of the recovery make the case for action perfectly clear: Women face structural barriers that have made them more vulnerable to the pandemic's impacts, and eliminating these barriers will jumpstart the recovery," Melinda wrote in a blog post. The Gates Foundation subsequently pledged $330 million to improving the workplace for women, increasing their financial station, and opening leadership opportunities up to them.[1]

BIAS IN AI LEADS TO BIAS IN OPPORTUNITY

In 2019, after leading Minor Guard for a year, I exited into a larger player in the child safety software market, Bark Technologies. Two years later, I became a management consultant on data strategy. Back in 2015, I did not know what the term AI stood for, but I became energized by seeing how much progress was being made by using it in precision medicine for cancer treatment.

By leveraging personally identifiable information about patient data, doctors were able to substantially improve the outcomes for thousands of patients that participated in the Collaborative Cancer Cloud project between Oregon Health and Science University, MIT, and Harvard leveraging confidential computing for recommending the best precision medicine treatment for the patient. Embracing AI for digital transformation can turn oceans of data into pearls of wisdom.

One coworker of mine was diagnosed with an aggressive form of cancer and was given six months to live. By leveraging this AI solution, his treatment team was able to identify the best course of treatment to get him into remission, and he is still thriving seven years later.

In regulated industries like healthcare, that data is often not used to its full potential due to security risks. In order to allow machines to do what they do uniquely well (repetitive tasks, math, pattern recognition) and humans to do what they do uniquely well (investigation and intuitions), it is important to keep up with digital transformation to accelerate precision medicine and reduce bias. I have focused my career on AI for Good in order to bring influential leaders and innovation together to address social justice issues at scale.

Data science has revealed a lot of systemic issues in the workplace that have been there for a long time. Unfortunately, bias in AI is not just bias; it's bias at scale. I'm sure we've all encountered an individual who we felt was biased in their response to us. Now imagine if you could take that one hiring manager and encode their problematic attitude into an algorithm that is applied to thousands of people.

We have a lot of things we need to be cautious about as we move forward with this new technology. I think the answer comes down to the people we have leading and building these solutions. That is why it is crucial to increase diversity in this space. The more diverse minds we have in the conversations, designing, developing, creating, and leading the solutions, the better the outcomes will be for companies and society in the long term.

In a job interview process, for example, just repeating patterns that led to successful candidates will not yield results that accelerate equity. Those past hiring decisions were inherently biased by the human beings making the decisions. To be human is to be biased, and data science is only as good as the data you feed the algorithm. If we don't have a broader perspective from the people in the room, if we don't make a *human* change, we're going to continue to leave behind a lot of the people.

Increasing diversity in data careers became a passion of mine after seeing the impact of AI bias at scale. This can be seen in gender bias for candidate screening software and racial bias in predatory loan advertisements. This is a unique opportunity to break the cycle of generational poverty through education and access to the dignity of a paycheck in technology careers.

Women in Data is a community of over thirty thousand people with representation in fifty-five countries. The founder and CEO, Sadie St. Lawrence, states, "Technology . . . is a common language between countries." Women in Data first makes people aware of the opportunities in tech and data science; they may never have been exposed to its possibilities before. Then they educate and upskill the new potential workforce. St. Lawrence says, "Fifty percent of the population will need upskilling by 2025 just to deal with the rapid change in technology." Women in Data is addressing that need with a variety of education, residency, and mentorship programs to provide the necessary skills for these populations who would traditionally be left out of the industry.

This leads to a feedback loop. Marian Wright Edelman wrote for the Children's Defense Fund in 2015: "From an awareness standpoint, we live in our own vacuum of information. . . . We have to be able to break out of this echo chamber to see the possibility of what's available and the possibility of what jobs and roles are available for you in technology. . . . 'It's hard to be what you can't see.'"[2]

By looking past the biased algorithms created by biased humans and based on biased human interactions, we can expand the field of candidates. This inclusion creates a diversity of experience and thought, which leads to innovation and generally better outcomes for everyone involved.

"I worked for a global tech company that kept building its products and services around its own core technology instead of building around technology the rest of the world was using. Over and over I witnessed this tunnel vision, perpetuated by hubris and a lack of thought diversity. The inability to look outside our own walls and understand the evolving market and the consumer led to flopped launches, fizzled mergers, failed product lines, and flat-lined stock growth. Under new leadership, this company is back on track today, but those were painful years for employees and shareholders."

—Sheryl

Melinda Gates puts it well: "Society puts things on women, puts things on people of color, and you don't see those role models in those high positions—A young man looks up, . . . and he sees three dozen different archetypes of men."

She continues, "People think we are fifty or sixty years away from equality in America. And the truth is we are over two hundred years from equality, when you look at all the measurements of when somebody's reached equality."[3]

UPSKILLING AND SAFE SPACES TO FAIL

We have entered the data and AI age, making business leaders indispensable. Around 90 percent of all data was created in the last two years, propelling the Internet into the zettabyte era. By 2025, 463 million terabytes will be created every day. The trends of consumerization require a new skill set as 80 percent of that data is unstructured and can only be understood at scale with a robust data platform and automation.

Russ Whitman, chief strategy officer at Launch Consulting, said that AI is being used to "deliver more personalized solutions for both customers and employees," but "we are starting to see the big leaps forward rather than incremental changes for companies." These big leaps will require a big leap in skilled workers. "I think it's this shift [from] innovation groups—in a CIO or CTO team—to where the business leaders are exploring. How can I leverage AI and machine learning to better understand my population and deliver the right services that they need? Especially now that we've been forced to transform how we work every day, resulting in accelerated digital transformation year."

Awareness is key in helping women see that they can have a career in a high-paying data role. From there, we worked to educate and upskill; today, it's estimated that 50 percent of the population will need upskilling by 2025 just to deal with the rapid change in technology. To do so, we will need a variety of programs—learning pathways, residency programs, and mentorship—to bring the community together but, more importantly, to provide the right skills.

Failure is the price of admission for innovation, so having a space where people from marginalized groups feel true inclusion and psychologically safe to take risk is key. In order to find the best solutions, humans often need to be able to cocreate, which requires trust, respect, and building on each other's ideas. This all comes back to inclusion: A diverse workforce is a win–win for everyone.

> "Women represent over half of the global population and in the US, they influence 90 percent of all purchasing decisions. Yet only about 19 percent of industrial engineers or product designers are women. Without enough women influencing product design, we will continue to design for a man's world—think about what this means in the design for watch chargers, shoe design, safety equipment, tool design, automobiles . . . the list goes on and on."
>
> **—Lisa**

THE DARK SIDE OF TECH

Although equity and inclusion are crucial for any innovative company, as an individual, you must also work toward your own personal purpose. Without greater meaning in your work, it can sap your energy and tip your work and life toward burnout.

I have had the benefit of opportunities to work in the STEM field since 2000. Let me tell you about the time Ashton Kutcher blew my mind. He was leading a product development discussion and planning for the brightest software tech minds at the Thorn industry event in 2016 in San Francisco. I was new to the trust and safety engineering community and looking for ways that Intel could support the fight to end child sexual abuse material and human trafficking. This was the first time I got to connect with brilliant technologists, including Travis Bright, Federico Gomez, and Roopal MacDuff, who became long-term mentors of mine over the years.

I had no idea Kutcher would actually be leading a four-hour meeting for a room of forty subject matter experts. He is wicked smart and fully devoted to this cause. I was so impressed, I got situationally shy and never introduced myself. He went as far as doing the voiceover for the closing keynote video at OpenSummit 2017, which was based on my team's work, and I am always inspired by his commitment and contribution to the cause.

A month later, I was back at Google headquarters to meet with the trust and safety experts across the industry to explore tool development for better proactive identification of illegal content on platforms and processes to remove it more quickly from distribution. Many companies were represented in the room, including Microsoft, Intel, Palantir, and Facebook (now Meta). After we wrapped our two-day industry face-to-face, a small group of us was huddled at the conference room table, chatting. We were discussing who had the data to train an AI model for effective detection of the age of a minor in an explicit image.

A lawyer in the room said, "Not only do parents upload images from birth onward, but they label them for the company by tagging the images. By the time a child turns eighteen, this company will know every friend they have, where they go, and who their family is. Any parent who posts pictures of their kids may deeply regret that in the future." I sat back in my chair and realized for the first time "guilty as charged"; I too have done my share of "sharenting."

Following that event, I was invited by Yiota Souras down to Los Angeles for a documentary film premier for *I Am Jane Doe* by Mary Mazzio, which features her. Yiota Souras is the VP of legal and VP of trafficking at the National Center for Missing and Exploited Children. Attending movie premiers was not part of my typical day as a tech worker, so I was excited to be in the room with John Walsh (founder of NCMEC and host of *America's Most Wanted*) and decided to make the trip. I expected to see all the folks I had met at the Thorn event but was surprised when I arrived to discover that Yiota had only invited two people: me and her brother.

Every other person in that theater was a lawyer who had represented a teenage victim of human trafficking pro bono against Backpage.com for their profiting from their abuse. These lawyers had all lost their cases due to a law from 1996, the Communications Decency Act 230, which gave platforms immunity from responsibility for third-party content. During the film, Mary Mazzio (the documentary's director), explores the paper trail and discovers that many of the large technology companies were funding the Backpage's defense to the tune of hundreds of millions of dollars. (According to the documentary, $150 million had been spent by Google alone.) I left uncomfortable but activated to use my position of power to do something to support these children. This law was being reviewed for updating under the Stop Exploiting Sex Trafficking Act, which was miraculously passed into law a year later by Congress.

When I attended the Hope Awards in Washington, DC, later that year, I was seated at the table with Yiota and Mary while they received their awards for being the most impactful in this space for that year. I leaned over to Yiota and whispered into her ear, "It is such an honor for me to be here with you tonight. May I ask why I was the only person from the industry you invited to join you for the film premier?"

She replied, "I sensed you truly care about this and have an important role in this movement to play, like I do."

I nodded, but it was not clear where I could add value.

Mary called me shortly after I arrived back home to ask what I could do to encourage Intel to take a stand on changing this law.

I replied, honestly, that I didn't know, but I was willing to explore and find out.

With the help of my executive sponsors, Lisa Davis and Bob Rogers, I kicked off on a one-year tour, taking the Intel jet to multiple states to meet with company executives face-to-face to better educate them about the issues of human trafficking and online child sexual abuse material. I also asked them to join us in committing resources to developing AI software, modernizing NCMEC's data center, and providing government affairs support to explore ways Section 230 could be modernized to address the loophole. I explained that it provides immunity to criminals who are profiting from crimes against women and children; companies can continue to profit while they are aware that there are children being exploited on their platforms. After many miles, presentation, and conversations, we reached alignment, and Intel was ready to move forward.

In 2017, I co-led Intel's partnership with the NCMEC, where I learned the facts about the growth of reports of child sexual abuse material. I'm not talking about risqué schoolgirl photos; I'm talking about reports of crime scene photos of child victims shared for enjoyment. The problem grew from five hundred thousand in 2013 to over 21.7 million in 2020. With the problem scaling so fast, NCMEC's team of analysts could not keep up. They needed to determine where each case needed to be sent for law enforcement follow up, but there was a thirty-day turnaround time for any case not marked *urgent*.

We set a goal of helping them to use AI to accelerate the coordinated national response from within thirty days to within twenty-four hours of reports of abuse. Our team of engineers, data scientists, and project managers created a solution that went into production in 2018. To accomplish this goal, we needed to create custom algorithms to recommend where in the world an image was likely accessed to accelerate coordination with the right law enforcement agency. This eliminated a lot of manual work the analysts were doing with IP addresses to find when a criminal made a mistake and gave away their location. Machines were able to do the tedious, repetitive work, and humans were freed up to do the investigation and analysis that made the reports actionable to recover victims. It took a year of work, and I have never felt more proud of a team's contribution to actually addressing a social problem with our work, rather than just philanthropy.

We learned a lot during the process about how to apply digital transformation for highly sensitive datasets. We had to figure out what workloads made sense to run in the cloud and what must stay on premises and how to leverage the data for more insights to accelerate outcomes.

Working inside the system for ten years, I became aware that many technology innovations were funded or accelerated by the pornography industry. They were the first to accept payments online, they drove more content streaming than ESPN and Disney combined, and the beta versus VHS wars were won by pornography signing the contract with VHS for distribution. One day in LA, while selling solid state drives for content streaming to a large media company, I was interrupted during my technical explanation of how a system architecture redesign could improve their cost while delivering content by a VP who said, "Can we just cut to the chase? We are not solving world hunger here. We are just getting the porn to the people faster."

This customer had no idea that, on my nights and weekends, I was trying to eliminate human trafficking, which is accelerated by the pornography industry. This was the first indication in 2017 that made me question whether I could continue working in corporate America.

The final straw came later that year when I was working with government affairs to support new legislation to revise the Communications Decency Act Section 230 to remove blanket immunity from technology platforms for the sale of human trafficking victims on their platforms. Backpage.com was facing charges from the States of California and Texas for knowingly facilitating the sale of victims on their platform. As a neutral technology player and initial party involved in convening the 1996 legislation, Intel was interested in getting all the parties together to help accelerate common-sense language that would keep the intentions of CDA 230 intact while not allowing immunity from prosecution to companies who were facilitating blatantly illegal transactions. Backpage, for example, hosted the sale of over 1,700 minors for sex up to twenty times a day in the US alone, according to NCMEC's reviews. Intel set forward to convene the major tech players to close this loophole.

Once I gained agreement from our leadership, which took months of education and coordination to get approved, I excitedly called Mary Mazzio to let her know we were making progress. My enthusiasm was extinguished a couple of weeks later, when one of Intel's largest customers placed a call to the head of government affairs. They said, "If Intel decides to take a neutral or positive position on this legislation, there would be significant impacts to their business relationships," and that he would call the CEO to explain why. At that moment, the project was stopped, and I was notified we would not be getting involved.

The reason technology companies did not want this to move forward was not that they wanted human trafficking to persist. Rather, they had no business incentive to do more than was required of them by the law. In order to be more vigilant, they would need to add content moderation staff, and if their platform was in any way used for illegal activity, even without their knowledge, they would face potential lawsuits from victims, who could prove they profited from their victimization through ad revenue.

That was the last straw for me, if we could not all agree that the rape of children was an unacceptable cost of doing business, I was taking my ball and moving to a new field. To bring it back to the value of inclusion, this mercenary approach to business might not be as prevalent if people from broader backgrounds were in leadership. It is why I think we need more representation of women on boards and the C-suite of technology. We need to look beyond revenues and invest in programs to derisk companies from third-party user-generated content. Business as usual is no longer acceptable.

"I hope people stop underestimating people that don't look like them. I hope I've proven that women and Latinas are great stewards of capital and managers of businesses. People told me that less than 2 percent of venture capital goes to women and people of color and to NOT start a company. We've raised over six million dollars for Caribu—don't let people tell you what you can't do!"

—Max

"When I was a VP at a large tech firm, I was among a very small group of women at that level (about 280 women in a company of over one hundred thousand). I was new, in an atypical role for the company—a creative versus an engineer. I was also gay. I was at dinner on more than one occasion when a really offensive homophobic conversation would pop up. I would listen and wait and when they were finished I'd explain that I was gay. I'd excuse myself to the bathroom to let the Senior VPs regain their composure and return to get a less than heartfelt apology. My team (which was one of the MOST diverse groups in the company) was eventually cut. I mistakenly showed some emotion when I was informed in a public meeting that my team was being eliminated. The next day my female boss shamed me, telling me my reaction was unacceptable. She went on to tell me I needed to shape up and prove that I wanted to be there. After that lashing I didn't want to be there and left as did many women."

—Teresa

INTERSECTIONALITY

"Systems of inequality are interrelated. Whether they are based on race, ethnicity, sexual orientation, gender identity, disability, or any other characteristic, forms of discrimination intersect to create complex results, behaviors, and biases."[4]

As a disabled woman in the workplace, I found that my psychological safety in the workplace was often disrupted by someone with more power than me who was not behaving with integrity. When you fit into more than one category that, by themselves, are tested by societal bias, they can compound. People with intersectional vulnerabilities are already working harder than most to contribute and to be valued for their contributions. There is more isolation, more headwind, and more required effort to be included on the team, not just represented.

The myth that the workplace will work for women if we all just "lean in" or work on our "executive presence" is another way corporate America has been able to focus all the work of achieving equity back onto women instead of changing the patriarchal culture that prevents them from succeeding in leadership roles.

My grandmother passed away when I was three years old after having had a low quality of life for many years from a combination of the trauma of losing her parents, home, and life during World War II. I was raised in an environment that highly valued education, because it could never be taken away from you, and that encouraged saving money to be prepared for an emergency. But I was also raised with the legacy of my grandparents' and parents' lives as stateless refugees: a constant fear that such an emergency—and the danger that comes with it—could be around every corner.

"I'm awakened now, whereas I might've been sleepwalking before. And that might surprise some people to hear because I was at the height of my career, so it begs the question, 'how can you be in hustle-mode, doing great at work, and sleep-walking at the same time?' But, when you are in hustle mode for things that are out of alignment with your core purpose, you're still sleeping, just sleep-running, instead of sleepwalk-ing. I have always had the audacity to make my own way, defy the odds, and follow my inner wisdom. I had the audac-ity to skip the four-year college route and join the US Air Force Intelligence squadron at nineteen, continue my college degree online while deployed for war, and in 2018—when representation didn't matter to most—I had the audacity to create and executive produce *Soci Circle* (a diverse tween web series) with zero filmmaking experience. Six months later, the show won a Hollywood film festival."

—Tiana

Although I have benefitted from privilege and had access to a high-quality education, I do know firsthand how diffi-cult being different can be and how taxing that feeling can be on your efforts to succeed in a chosen career, not to mention how a lack of role models and sponsors can derail someone's career over time. But I also know that, for many people, the corporate world offers much tougher challenges than just a lack of appropriate role models. People belonging to a myriad of marginalized groups face unspoken biases and obstacles in the workforce every day, and the insidious pervasiveness of these perspectives can be hard to believe unless you have lived the same experiences.

NAVIGATING FORWARD

- We are still two hundred years away from equity for women in America without intervention today.

- The price of admission for innovation is failure. People need a safe space to experiment and grow, if that is the outcome we want.

- Corporations are not social services organizations. There may come a time where your vision and the goals of the company diverge, and that is a sign that perhaps you would be a better fit somewhere else.

- Everyday people can be career saving for marginalized people when they choose to use their power to support the victim at an individual level.

CAREER REBOOT ACTION: IDENTIFY YOUR VALUES

Write down your personal values: What is most important to you? Living your values by creating a unique, purposeful mission eases your path forward. Your personal values will help you identify the life that uniquely aligns with who you want to be, what you want to do, and the legacy you want to leave behind. Your values will change over time, as will your priorities; reassess them periodically.

CHAPTER 9

Healthcare Not Sick Care

When COVID-19 was declared a pandemic, we were all instructed to shelter in place. The hospital system did not have the capacity to treat another wave of patients all at once. There was not enough personal protective equipment for frontline workers, and medical professionals were literally putting their lives and the lives of their families on the line to save others. With staffing and bed shortages becoming the norm for emergency rooms globally, many nurses have been worked beyond burnout and are opting out of the field. It is not uncommon for doctors and nurses to be in situations where there are not enough beds for patients, mental health facilities for people in crisis, or staff to coordinate care for complex cases. This is particularly hard on frontline doctors and nurses. The functional medicine and wellness industries

"Healthcare has more representation of women than many other sectors. However, we continue to lose women to the workforce because of the lack of infrastructure and support for women, including affordable childcare, paid family leave, flexible working hours, equal pay and commitment to inclusion."

—Lisa

have risen to meet this gap at a significant out-of-pocket cost to patients. This is a stopgap alternative when those patients can't get answers from their traditional medicine providers, who often only have fifteen minutes to see them.

But COVID just put front and center struggles in the healthcare industry that have existed for a long time. Women make up the majority of nursing staff required for patient care. And many female doctors in healthcare feel the same barriers to entry for leadership positions in their field as are reflected in the technology sector. In addition, women have not been the primary focus of medical research, and the ways that diseases are diagnosed and treated tend to be from a male perspective.

In December 1999, I had just graduated from the University of Michigan's School of Engineering. I had an offer in hand to move out to Silicon Valley that January to begin my career in the tech industry. Being so close to Y2K, all the news and chatter that month was about what IT and banking infrastructure was going to break when the year flipped to 2000.

I was staying with my best friend, Anna, for a few weeks between apartment leases. Through her, I was witness to the largest heartbreak one can experience in this life, the loss of a

"In departments, in hospital administration leadership, and in state/national groups, leadership is still mostly male, which limits opportunities for same-gender mentorship and guidance from those who have come before. This is slowly changing, but I have sat in plenty of meetings in which I am very conscious of the fact that I am in the minority as a woman, or in which I note that all senior leadership is male. In meetings, male physicians are more likely to be called by their title (e.g., Dr. Smith) and female physicians by their first names (e.g., Jenny). Even in patient care, bias is present . . . patients often assume that female physicians are nursing staff (either referring to the female physician by their first name or as their nurse and/or later complaining that they never saw a physician), lack the authority to make decisions, or vocalize assumptions based upon physical appearance—the physician is too young, old, pretty, weak, etc.—to accomplish the job at hand."

—Sara

parent. Anna's mother passed away due to complications from a brain tumor on New Year's Eve—days before I was to leave for the West Coast.

Her mom had made many trips to doctors in 1998, complaining of severe headaches. As a trained pharmacist, she knew something was not right. Over and over again, she was sent home with a speech about reducing her stress or with instructions on how to manage menopause symptoms with Tylenol. On her third trip to the doctor, her husband refused to leave the ER without an MRI. That scan revealed a softball-sized brain tumor. The day before I left for California, I attended her funeral and left Anna alone to cope with losing her mother at the age of twenty-one.

Unfortunately, not much has changed since 1999. As recently as 2020, this kind of dismissal by (usually male) medical professionals of legitimate patient concerns is called *medical gaslighting*. When doctors and medical professionals downplay symptoms and complaints, like they did with Anna's mom, we start to feel crazy and doubt our body's signals. I now have personal experience about how difficult and frustrating it can be to navigate the medical system in this country as a woman.

I am Ashlie, a cancer survivor, and for the past thirty-two years I have learned what it means to advocate for myself in our healthcare system. At twenty-four years old I was four months into my marriage and received the cancer diagnosis one does not want to hear. I will never forget the first doctor I saw at Duke Medical Center. He was young, confident, and came into the room with a long needle ready to aspirate my tumor. No discussion, no explanation. Just follow his advice and allow him to stick this long needle into my throat to get cells to be tested for cancer.

I remember feeling completely overwhelmed at the fact he thought I had cancer—no one had mentioned that yet—and he wanted no discussion. He came to do what he wanted to do. I froze. My husband asked the doctor the purpose of the aspiration, to which he scoffed, "It is normal procedure to test for cancer cells." What I do remember is my husband grabbing my hand and walking out of the room. I don't remember much of what else transpired in that moment except that I was sad and confused. Why did this doctor not answer my husband's question and why did he

continued →

think I had cancer? Where would we go next? Duke Medical Center was the premier healthcare institution in the area.
How could I find a doctor I could trust and would listen? I felt
small and unworthy that day.

The good news was that I did find a doctor who came
out of part-time retirement and did my cancer surgery. He
was sixty-four years old when he rolled me into the operating room, removed my cancer, and was a dear friend until he
died in 2014. He often shared with me that I needed to be
my own advocate. He shared that the health system could
be complicated to navigate, and advocacy was key to getting the treatment I needed. So, from the age of twenty-four
I began my journey of advocacy. Over the past thirty-two
years I have learned so much and have had to advocate
through many doctors who looked past me and felt they
knew better what I needed than I knew myself.

I know what was best for me and my health. It is not
easy sometimes pushing back, in fact, it is uncomfortable
and makes me feel uneasy, but speaking up and advocacy
is using your own voice for you.

Since I was diagnosed with a rare form of vasculitis and long
COVID in 2021, I have lost count of the number of specialists
I have seen and the amount of invasive testing I have endured to
better understand what it will take to reduce the symptoms of
my gastrointestinal issues, back pain, and chronic fatigue. Without a proper diagnosis, I have been released from the emergency
room multiple times with potentially life-threatening issues. I
have been told I don't look sick enough for hospitalization or
further tests.

In my field, I can command a room, yet as a patient in pain,

I present like a woman who may be self-diagnosing on Google. It is such a dramatic juxtaposition to spend the morning advising the head cardiologist at a world-leading medical research institution on how to use AI to transform healthcare and the afternoon with a rheumatologist who asked, "Where did you get your medical degree?" when I dared to ask for testing to confirm a disease I would later be diagnosed with.

After a decade-long mystery, I can't explain the relief I had to finally receive a diagnosis and treatment options beyond "reducing stress" this year. I recognize my privilege to have the support of my family and employer and the resources to be able to manage reasonably well despite not feeling well or being healthy. However, there were many times I started to believe that maybe it was all in my head after testing failed to reveal the source of my pain. With a diagnosis, I am much better able to understand my triggers, my limitations, and how to pace myself.

As a result of the countless stories from other women and my own experience, I truly understand the need to reduce bias in healthcare. I am committed to relentlessly advocating for marginalized people's right to physical and mental health in order for them to thrive. Many marginalized groups have experienced implicit bias in healthcare, beyond what I have experienced as a privileged white woman, and I am committed to accelerating the clinical use of AI to complement doctors' lived experience in order to help with diagnosis, recovery, and patient outcomes.

My background as an entrepreneur and consultant provides me with the experience to help companies focus on immediate and incremental value, learning and adapting, and finding the right people and partners to drive innovation. In leading Launch's

Data for Good Practice, I helped raise the first million dollars for a medical research institute to define a product roadmap for a startup to accelerate AI decision support tools for doctors in clinical settings to improve care. Part of this includes reducing bias in models to ensure they perform as well on a middle-aged man in India as they do for an elderly woman in Indiana. Today's companies do not have a shortage of vision, but there is often a shortage of knowing *how to get there*.

Although AI simplifies lives and makes things more convenient, it is important that we accelerate diversity in all areas of leadership and product development. Safeguarding personal, proprietary, and sensitive data is also important. Companies often effectively lock it up and throw away the key, but that data could catapult your business to greater success—if you could use it securely. We aren't just talking about making money. We're talking about curing cancer. We're talking about predicting the next global pandemic. We're talking about changing the future for ourselves and for our children.

In 2019, I met with Dr. Michael Blum, the chief digital transformation officer at the University of California, San Francisco (UCSF) and the executive director at UCSF's Center for Digital Healthcare Innovation. He said, "Today, it takes millions of dollars and several years to access and compute on the sensitive patient data needed for an FDA approval of an AI model that runs in a clinical setting. We created IP that can cut the time and cost in half. If we do this right, we can improve patient outcomes and reduce missed diagnoses." The thought that we could address the known bias in healthcare with a digital transformation to better support marginalized groups drives my mission.

Medical errors cost approximately $20 billion a year and approximately one hundred thousand lives.[1] That is not counting the missed diagnoses or injuries from medication that are common in outpatient settings. I have yet to meet a doctor that goes to work intending to make an error that could cost someone their life. But with time pressure, cost efficiency measures, and intrinsic biases, sometimes these errors occur.

In 2020, Michael's company, Beekeeper AI, and Launch Consulting set a goal of creating the technology roadmap for a two-sided marketplace, where data stewards (research hospitals, academics) securely provide data to algorithm owners (startups, medical device manufacturers, and academics) to accelerate model validation and training on more diverse datasets without ever moving the data. In order to accomplish this goal, we need to create custom solutions for confidential computing with a frictionless user experience. We are trying to give access to diverse medical data while maintaining the intellectual property of healthcare systems. Allowing machines to take over some of this work in model validation will let doctors focus more time on their patients. It took a year of work. I am extremely proud to be a part of this team—knowing that in a few years, we will all know someone who was diagnosed earlier and whose life was saved because of the work we are doing today.

When we started this project, the total number of novel AI models with Food and Drug Administration approval for clinical settings was six. And hundreds of thousands of models are awaiting enough data for validation and approval. The team that got the first official model approved in partnership with GE was the UCSF Center for Digital Healthcare Innovation.

Half of the leadership team of practicing physicians noticed that having the right data at the right time could save lives.

The first use case we explored was a traumatic car accident. We used AI to help determine whether the victim would need a blood transfusion. There are a few markers that indicate that the patient will bleed out on the operating table without this intervention. The challenge is that it happens in a matter of minutes, but it takes time to prep the right blood for transfusion. AI can determine whether the patient is in a risk category, which allows the doctors to focus on repairing the trauma surgically while the rest of the team can get the order to the blood bank immediately.

From this initial use case, we expanded to testing the long-term effects of COVID-19 on lung damage for patients that had recovered from the original infection. Here, the model uses imaging data to provide better treatment and monitoring protocols. From there, the next use case was using diabetic retinopathy imaging to determine from an image taken during an eye exam screening whether a patient was likely developing diabetes, in order to treat it early before permanent damage is done. These are a couple of examples of the early use cases, but the bigger picture is that doctors are human and can only manage so much information at a time. With AI models that can be used in clinical settings, we no longer need to rely solely on intuition and experience to find patients at an increased risk for serious complications.

This is especially important as the medical frontline workforce is required to do more with less and is experiencing burnout and suicidal ideation at a rate many times higher than the average work population. A female ER doctor friend of mine shared that, due to her profession, she is statistically forty times more likely than the average person to commit suicide. The contributing factors to this situation include burnout, high student loans, and a lack of support staff to help doctors and nurses to meet the needs of the patients they have. In 2022, she shared that it is now common for her to have more than eighty patients awaiting treatment, but her ER only has thirty beds. On some shifts, her job is to literally scan the ER waiting room to assess which patient she thinks will die if they are not tended to next.

"Patient volumes are high," she says, "EMS stretchers line up in front of our desks like small, tragic train cars from some war zone. On them, old men and women slump in exhaustion or cry from broken bones. On others, young addicts struggle against restraints because of their methamphetamine use or scream because Narcan robbed them of their high; saving their lives causes instant and miserable withdrawal." These patients are left to wait in the hallways while the staff desperately tries to find rooms to put them in.[2]

Many of her patients requiring mental health support are being held in the ER for days or weeks due to a lack of beds for inpatient treatment. Her working hours also fluctuate between day and night, sometimes within the same week, making sleep very difficult or impossible. In addition, she has elementary-school-age children and is the breadwinner of the family. It is impossible for her to take a sabbatical or even a vacation.

This level of fatigue and constant performance is where mistakes are made. Empathy fatigue sets in not just for the doctors but for the public hearing these stories. We are letting down our frontline workers. Medicare and insurance reimbursements often don't account for any coordination of care, funding for upskilling on new treatments, or any additional time needed when the patient's symptoms do not fit those typical of middle-aged white men, where the majority of medical research has been focused. With the lack of nursing staff, the lack of foresight in building enough hospitals to address population growth and aging, retiring physicians, the lack of primary care, and the fact that about half of all American healthcare happens in the ER, no wonder our healthcare professionals are struggling.[3]

It is so important to accelerate innovation in healthcare so that we can reduce bias and improve patient outcomes, and do it in a cost-effective way that makes it sustainable and scalable. This will require innovation, investment, and commitment in order to secure our system for future generations.

NAVIGATING FORWARD

- We need to look at restructuring healthcare for sustainability after the pandemic.

- Burnout is not only happening in corporate America; it is happening for frontline workers at alarming rates.

- The cost of turning healthcare into a business has come at the expense of the mental and physical health of our caregivers.

- Medical professionals have the highest suicide rate of any profession.

- Nursing shortages are expansive, because we are not taking mental health into account for retention strategies.

CAREER REBOOT ACTION:
REBOOT BEFORE BURNOUT

If you feel stuck in a toxic environment, remember that you have to get out of that system before you can start to heal from the effects it is having on you. Consider a medical leave, if it is available, to work on your burnout without triggers that may set you back.

CHAPTER 10

The Role of Male Allies

"A rising tide lifts all boats."
—John F. Kennedy

We don't have to do it all alone. Everyone who creates a career legacy has sponsors and mentors along the way that aid in getting the resources, alignment, and commitment to bring their vision into reality. That's been a cornerstone of the business world since the dawn of time. And men can be an important ally to women in the tech industry and beyond.

When you gain clarity on your vision and mission and start to talk about it, you never know who will be drawn to helping you bring it to fruition. When I started focusing on using AI to disrupt human trafficking, I was limited in who I thought would be interested in my journey. Given that it seemed like

"I started to understand that a mindset shift had to happen in order for my life to improve. My dad, understandably tired of all my whining and crying, lovingly shook me by the shoulders and said, 'You can't work for other people and there's no shame in that.' Eureka! The next day, my husband bought me Guy Kawasaki's *Art of the Start*. Somewhere in the first few pages, it reads: 'Don't make a plan, just get started.' The day after that, I just happened to go to a business lunch with two incredible humans who turned out to be angel investors. They gave me $50,000 to start my first company."

—Kate

work toward a societal good, I thought more women than men would be interested in volunteering. I was wrong. Not only did more men connect with that mission, but most of my core team members were men who passionately cared about better protecting women and children in the world. Don't underestimate the power of a compelling mission to get people mobilized, and take care not to be gender biased and assume that men won't want to be involved.

As a female founder, I am struck by the statistic that only 2.2 percent of venture capital is provided to female founders. When I was doing a seed round for my startup Minor Guard, we used a mix of sweat equity and founder funding, and we had the benefit of an angel investor that helped us get the first $200,000 to complete our corporate entity formation, create our minimum viable product, and get our first proof of concept completed. We were able to merge with a larger player in the market before moving to our next stage, which allowed us to accelerate our time to market for getting solutions to help prevent the creation of child sexual abuse material online. Since our angel investor was so key in going from ideation to execution, I wanted to share his perspective on why he chose to invest in a first-time female founder, so others with excellent company ideas may find paths to funding.

Gregg Descheemaeker provided the seed funding to make the vision Hasan and I set out on a reality. He also served on Minor Guard's board of directors and helped me build out the team to go from a dream to a company. Hasan and Gregg each represent the two things founders need—someone to help bring women to the table where decisions are being made and more people that just see business skills when they look at business people.

Gregg was asked, "Why invest in a woman-owned startup?"[1] His answer was one I wanted the world to hear: "There are a LOT of attractive business investments out there to bet on, so I choose to invest in areas where I have experience and knowledge, a strong personal interest, and finally, I'm a firm believer in investing in opportunities that have people I believe in, whom I think can fundamentally compete at a different level than the peers they'll go head-to-head with in the marketplace."

Gregg said he focuses on two aspects of any company he's considering investing in. First, the company: Is its purpose in line with Gregg's values? In our case, we were a tech startup focused on combatting child pornography, sextortion, and cyberbullying using artificial intelligence. Our application to smartphones—literally in the child's hands—had the potential to be a huge differentiator and could really help protect kids. This mission was something Gregg was interested in getting engaged with and doing more for.

Lee Christofferson

Gregg Descheemaeker, myself, and Mahmudul Hasan
at my presentation to 2020 Women on Boards.

Second, Gregg looks at the leadership of the company. That was me.

Gregg said, "Lisa Thee was founding this company, some-one whom I'd met and worked with at Intel, I had personally worked with her and observed as she applied her entrepreneur-ial skills inside the walls of a large Fortune 50 company to help launch a new product category. She was smart, tenacious, and had that unique balance of technical and business acumen. Did I mention tenacious?"

"The deciding factor was the draw to invest in Lisa. As a per-son. As someone who I unshakably believed in. It had nothing to do with whether she was a woman or a man," Gregg said. "It had everything to do with the fact that she was an engineer but could outsell most anyone I'd met (including myself). It had to do with the fact that she was demonstrating an incredible ability to transform an entire market and was getting recognized for her efforts on the national stage. And it had to do with the fact that, while she lacked direct experience of starting and leading a company, there was zero doubt in her dogged determination to outwork, outlearn, out-network, and outsell any competitor or challenge that might get in her way."

Investing in our company, where we were trying to do something that had never been done before, was risky. But Gregg saw past the risk to the much greater rewards: Minor Guard "presented the potential for both huge financial gain and the opportunity to positively impact something that I cared about deeply. It didn't seem like that much of a leap at all."

My company cofounder and brother Mahmudul Hasan passed away unexpectedly in July 2021 due to complications from COVID. He had helped me plan a panel called "Safety by Design for Web3" and was supposed to be a panelist. Instead, my nine-year-old son sat in Hasan's chair, because I was too grief-stricken to do it without his support. After the event, we went to Universal Studios to visit The Wizarding World of Harry Potter to celebrate Hasan's life. Hasan had bought tickets for us all to go together before he got sick, because he had wanted to share his love of the place with us.

In her book *Mean Baby: A Memoir of Growing Up*, Selma Blair says, "Every person on this earth needs just one person who sees them and roots for them. Deeply, truly. One person. It's what we all need to get through. The more the merrier, but let's start with one." Hasan was that person for me.

The last conversation I had with Hasan was when I shared

Blake Kuhre

My son sharing the stage with me at the NFT Expoverse.

with him that Fast Company agreed to publish this book that, for years, he had encouraged me to write. Hasan would have loved to be at my book signing for *Go!* He never craved the limelight but always loved seeing me shine. I asked him once why he did so much to support my dreams, and he shared that his biggest regret in life was not being able to sponsor his little sister to come to America from Bangladesh like he did for his brothers, who were now living the American dream. His sister married young and had responsibilities to take care of her husband and his parents, which never allowed her to fulfill her potential. Hasan said running Minor Guard with me inspired him to support women entrepreneurs. He launched and funded multiple companies with other woman after we exited.

In 2022, he returned to Apple in a new role as the global inclusion champion for Apple University. His team created training on how to better support women as male allies in tech, and he traveled to China, Colorado, and Ireland for the rollout. He called me when he got back, to personally thank me for inspiring him to dedicate his career to making it more just for women. He sponsored many women in tech, angel-invested in their companies, sat on their boards, and developed products to make them safer.

His daughter Morena is only two years old and will never have the chance to remember what a great man her father was. From rescuing a female reporter in Afghanistan from being murdered by the Taliban, to fixing the iPhone to better protect kids, to filming my TEDx talk, and doing my headshots for my website, Hasan's fingerprints are all over my career success. No idea was too big, no dream too lofty, and no setback too large to recover from. We all need those people in our corner that see our strengths and provide support when things are not going well. Find your people, and don't limit it to just people that look like you.

NAVIGATING FORWARD

- Talent is evenly distributed. We need to find ways to amplify the voices of marginalized groups in innovation. When we design for inclusion, everyone benefits.

- Look in your own network for the promising people you believe in that may need your support to rise to the occasion and lead.

CAREER REBOOT ACTION:
CONTROL WHAT YOU CAN

Plan and set goals and due dates. Look out into the future, and develop some new goals. Choose things that are within your control. Dream a bigger dream for yourself. What training can you take? What new skill can you learn?

PART 3

Your 90-Day
Career Reboot

CHAPTER 11

The Career Reboot Process

"Fight for the things you care about, but do it in
a way that will lead others to join you."

—Ruth Bader Ginsberg

When miners began sending a canary into the coal
mines to detect toxic levels of emissions before
entering themselves, the impact on the birds was
not their first concern. The canaries were a bellwether, a sensitive being that would react to toxicity much more quickly than
their human counterparts could. These sensitive creatures were
disposable in service of protecting the majority.

Being part of a marginalized group in society can feel like
being the canary, but you are also often told that, if you just
hold your breath long enough, the toxic fumes circulating in
the environment won't kill you. Management often provides

"Get curious and never stop wondering. As women we tend to think our way through feeling stuck. We vent to friends and family and it can feel too scary to take small action. Take the time to intentionally look at your life and career often, and especially when you start to feel 'stuck.' It's easy to be consumed by the daily grind and it's challenging to uncover the stories, thoughts, and feelings holding you back."

—Allison M.

guidance to people on how to behave differently in order to get better outcomes on their perceived performance vs. reflecting on the systems that favor groups with power who may be creating a toxic environment in the first place. But a toxic cloud will kill the canary every time. The skill of identifying that you are in a toxic environment and removing yourself as quickly as possible is the key to thriving. When you sense that toxicity, don't wait until you start to choke. Fly!

In her book *The Banish Burnout Toolkit*, Janice Litvin highlights that "Avoidance clues are a sure sign of burnout." Avoidance includes calling in sick so you don't have to deal with your abusive colleague. It might also show up as fatigue or anger. "The most obvious clue is an angry outburst at a loved one," Litvin observed. "Other clues include problems sleeping, feelings of resentment, and digestive issues."[1]

I have joked with other women leaders that the closest we get to a break is a dental visit, and some of my friends have even expressed a desire for solitary confinement for a weekend just to recharge. It is a sad state of affairs when one of the biggest fantasies for middle-aged women in the workforce is to be left alone.

> "Ask yourself what the worst thing that could happen might be. Chances are excellent that a change will not be the proverbial 'end of the world.' There are tons of ways to improve your career without having to throw out everything and the kitchen sink!"
>
> **—Sara**

CHANGING BEHAVIOR AND RESULTS

Mid- to late-career leadership can be lonely, challenging work. The door to success hinges on our creativity, our energy, and our resilience. I am a huge believer in actively building and participating in communities to buffer isolation. Although a commitment to change—a career reboot—may be necessary, you may not be ready for a full reboot right now. You can begin by adding self-care activities to your routine in order to move toward being ready.

WELLNESS PRACTICES

I have used wellness practices to address my own burnout and to prepare me to start my own reboot. Starting small, with little changes, you can build lifelong habits and increase your resilience. After we get through whatever difficult period we're in, we will be stronger and happier than we were before the changes.

Whether you are founding a new company, leaving or selling your current company, or staying to be part of a

continued →

transformation, here are some tactical tips to help you move
forward. You can refer back to the previous chapters for a
brief discussion of each tip.

- Build community
- Start an energy log
- Recharge
- Establish routines for self-care
- Restore joy and self-esteem
- Incorporate wellness practices that fit you
- Network
- Identify your values
- Reboot before burnout
- Control what you can

Although the career reboot process is independent work,
an accountability group is a wonderful way to share the journey with others in a way that supports better outcomes for
everyone. Consider creating a time for weekly check-ins on
progress as a team. Another option is to hire a career coach
to help you.

Changing your habits can put your willpower to the test. If
you find satisfaction in pushing yourself in your career, it can be
challenging to make time to take care of yourself and investigate
issues before they become emergencies.

As a recovering workaholic, I know my need to feel safe and
secure is tied up in financially providing for myself and my children. As with other addictions, it can feel compulsory to keep
going, no matter how tired you are. It is not viewed as shameful
to overwork in most societies, especially America. The challenge
can be that, by the time you realize something has to give, you

have already reached burnout. Change does not come overnight, and it is hard to motivate yourself to do something different when you are already operating in what feels like survival mode.

When I was in college, I was a pack-a-day smoker. When I started working, it was not as socially acceptable to smoke in California, so I set upon my journey to give it up. That journey was not a straight line, as it would turn out: For the next calendar year, I quit smoking and started again five times before I was able to really kick the habit. I would go through the withdrawal and feel the discomfort for weeks only to have a momentary lapse in judgment and light up a cigarette.

Eventually, I realized I was sick of going through withdrawal. If I kept giving myself excuses to go backward in my recovery, I would just be adding to the cycle of suffering. After four relapses, my fifth attempt stuck, and it has been twenty-two years since I touched a cigarette. That said, during the first six months of quitting, I thought about smoking all day long. For the second six months, it was the first thing I thought about when I woke up and the last thing before I went to bed at night. It took another year for my craving to abate, but I still thought about smoking weekly. Even more than twenty years later, I still dream about smoking from time to time. My feelings had to follow my actions, and I had to

"Move into something adjacent if you need to take smaller steps. e.g., similar role, different industry. The scariest part is just before you leap. Get going!"

—Sheryl

have faith and perseverance to sit with the discomfort for an extended period of time before I reaped the benefits of making healthier choices.

During the course of this experience, I have learned that some of the same skills that are used to break addiction to substances like nicotine apply well to changing an unhealthy relationship to work. I have distilled these tools and behaviors into a process I call the *career reboot*. This reboot has the power to transform your approach to work, reverse burnout, and set you on a new, more rewarding career path moving forward.

BUILD UP TO IT

Building habits takes time. It took me a long time to stop smoking. I had a goal and I had to recast my plan five times before I was able to give up the habit that wasn't serving me. The first few times I tried cold turkey which would last for a week or two before I caved to a craving. By the fifth time, I decided to use a nicotine patch to help me to reduce my intake more slowly while I worked on my mindset and coping skills. This is what allowed me to focus on what I wanted for my future in terms of health, and I developed patience to allow my cravings to pass without giving into them.

Building resilience is like building muscles. You must be consistent and thoughtful about the activities you undertake to see results. To prepare yourself to embark on the career reboot process, it is essential to reflect on your goals and the progress you are making, to ensure that the future you are building for yourself is one that meets your needs. The following tips may help you evaluate your goals and expectations going into your own career reboot:

- Get honest with yourself about the price you are paying right now for overcommitting (e.g., health, relationships, and spiritually).

- Identify what fear comes up for you at the thought of doing something different (e.g., finances, mission, or ego).

- Determine what you would be able to add to your life if you made more space for family, friends, and creativity.

- Recognize that new, healthier actions will always come before your old, unhealthy feelings and compulsions subside.

- Start a gratitude journal.

I have written a three-bullet gratitude journal for years, and I reflect on it annually. I write down three things that brought me joy that day before bed. After many years of this practice, I notice that most days are filled with simple moments with friends and family, rest, travel, and creative endeavors. It helps to ground me that my life is not defined by my career or my accolades, and my worth as a person is not on the line every day when I wake up. Over the course of time, the journal shows me the who, what, where, and when of moments of happiness I

"Shift from 'either/or' to 'AND' thinking. You will be surprised by the opportunities you can create!"

—JeanAnn

experience in my life, so that I can plan to spend more time in the places with people and animals that reconnect me to myself and renew my creativity.

TURNING PRACTICE INTO HABIT

During my college years, I started as a size two and graduated as a size fourteen. Going from a home where healthy homecooked meals were on the table every night to having the freedom to have pizza delivered at midnight led to some unexpected and unwanted pounds. I joined WeightWatchers at work and, following their plan, in three months I was able to lose the extra forty pounds I came to California with and then keep it off for a decade. I learned through that process that it takes about twenty-one days of practicing a change you want to make before it becomes a habit. To help you get habituated to new positive routines, you can try these ideas:

- Use your calendar to keep yourself accountable and control the number of hours you work.

- Get a buddy who is working on a similar goal but is a bit further along than you are. Their more established routine can help you get started.

- Try something new. A simple change may trigger a cascade of new habits.

- Create accountability. Check in with yourself and share your results with your friends.

> "Just because you don't know something doesn't mean you can't learn."
>
> —Heather

CONTROL WHAT YOU CAN

When I was asked to host a podcast, I was terrified! As a fan of them, I was not sure if I would cut it, and it required a new skill set. So I focused on what I did have, which was access to experts in a wide variety of fields, including cybersecurity, entrepreneurship, healthcare innovation, and data science. I knew that I always learned something when we connected for coffee, and I wanted to bring those interesting conversations to a larger audience. I focused on asking them questions that brought out their wisdom and a couple of actionable suggestions for each episode. Three seasons later, I was comfortable hosting. If you listen to *Navigating Forward* now, you will notice how the quality improves from the first episode. There were days in the first year I woke up in the middle of the night worried it would not turn out well, but I focused on what I could control, which was bringing interesting people on to share their expertise.

My friend Vikki was recovering from a car accident a few years ago. The wreck impaired her ability to walk due to a serious knee injury. Her first goal was simple: walk to her mailbox and back into her house. She then set a crazy goal: to walk two sections of the Portland to Coast walking relay. She had due

dates and subtasks for each goal. Today, Vikki competes globally in the Paralympic Games in fencing, which she picked up
after the accident. She no longer has to measure her progress
in distance, and even though her injury still affects her, she has
recovered her full quality of life.

THE REBOOT PROCESS

For the first twenty years of my career, I had stable corporate jobs. At the same time, I volunteered with organizations
that supported marginalized women and children to incorporate a sense of mission into my life. It was not something
I could dedicate forty hours a week to, because I was in the
career-building phase of my life, but I was able to balance
both without dropping balls. However, when the responsibilities of life started to add up and my career progressed, it was
no longer tenable to do both without negatively impacting
everything else. My drive and my ability to influence people
and get others on board with new ideas, combined with my
Type A personality, can make a me a force of nature when I set
my mind to something. It can also become my biggest liability
when I bite off more than I can chew. But it also means I can
stick to a process once it's begun.

The next steps required to cleanse your career are something
only you can define, but I have laid out some guidelines. I developed this process to take ninety days because it is the length of
a typical medical leave of absence. For many of my clients and
for me, it took a medical issue to prioritize redefining our career
portfolios. The body keeps score.

Month 1: Stabilize

- Week 1: Start an energy log
- Week 2: Take daily walks without looking at your phone
- Week 3: Meditate
- Week 4: Identify a unicorn space

Month 2: Dream

- Week 5: Reflect on your energy log
- Week 6: Identify your values
- Week 7: Network
- Week 8: Create a mission statement

Month 3: Plan

- Week 9: Lifestyle goals
- Week 10: Informational interviews
- Week 11: Don't accept the first offer
- Week 12: Persistence will pay off

Month 1: Stabilize

The goal of the first month of this process is to get out of your head and back into your body. To tune into your own inner wisdom, it is critical to tune out the noise of the world. After you achieve some success in your career, it becomes hard to separate your values from the values that are required to succeed at your job. In order to intentionally craft your career, it is important to return to what your dreams were for yourself, how they have evolved, and what skills you have developed.

The things that got you your current success will not necessarily get you where you want to go next, so it is important to be intentional about slowing down and feeling your feelings. Here is a week-by-week journaling exercise that can help you with accountability about listening to what your body has been trying to tell you.

WEEK 1: START AN ENERGY LOG

It is vital to start slowing down and not just keep pushing through your days in survival mode. The first step is awareness about how much energy you're expending trying to survive. Take five minutes a day and create a data log of how your energy ebbs and flows as you move through your tasks for the day. Note what activities and interactions drain you and which energize you. I recommend taking a few minutes at lunchtime and another couple of minutes before bed to document your tasks and feelings. Making that distinction is key to creating a life you will enjoy living.

We will use this data you create on Week 5 of this reboot, so please ensure you keep up the daily habit. Here are some prompts to help you observe your reactions to common scenarios:

- Do you find interacting with groups of people draining or energizing?

- Is there a meeting you dread or look forward to all week? What is it about that interaction that you can learn from?

- Do you feel like your interactions need to speed up or slow down?

- Is there an age group that you enjoy more (children, seniors, peers; do you enjoy leading more junior or senior teams)?

- Do you enjoy being the visionary or executing the vision as the operational leader?

- What makes your heart rate a bit faster in anticipation?

- What makes you want to crawl back into bed?

- What times of day do you have the most creativity?

- How many times did outside distractions take you off task?

What I noticed when I took the time to get out of my mind and back into my body was that procedural meetings with large groups of people drain my batteries quickly. I am more of a generalist than a specialist and don't prefer tedious detailed work. I also noticed that when I was providing one-on-one mentoring to people coming up in their career or advising established leaders, I almost never left a meeting without being more energized than when I arrived. When I had to sit in a conference room for more than two hours at a time, I would get bored and fidgety even if the topic was interesting. I think fast, move fast, and get impatient when I can't go at a comfortable speed. Finally, I noticed my creativity was highest in the morning and diminished as the day went on.

WEEK 2: TAKE DAILY WALKS
WITHOUT YOUR PHONE

One of the most healing things we can do for ourselves is exposure to nature. I like to take the time to notice the blue of the sky
and the tops of the trees. Over time, it is interesting to notice how
the landscape changes with the seasons and how, even on stressful
days, the birds are still flying, and the animals are still frolicking.
It is important to remember our place in this world: We don't
keep it spinning. We are a small part of a much bigger system that
will persist without us. This helps me to balance my instinct to
overfunction or take responsibility for things that I can't control.
I also function best with accountability, so I got a dog who needs
exercise as much as I do in order to motivate myself to stay consistent with my thirty- to sixty-minute daily walk.

WEEK 3: MEDITATE

It is important to build a daily practice of quiet time to observe
your thoughts. It can be challenging to build this muscle at
first, but it is important to tune into your breathing and learn
to observe your thoughts and feelings and notice how tran-
sient they are versus identifying with them. My journey toward
meditation was facilitated by the Headspace app. As a Type A
extrovert, I found guided meditation to be a good process to
ease slowing down and learning to observe.

Five years later, I have meditated over a thousand times for
an average of eleven minutes per session. When I am feeling
stuck or anxious, it is usually when I have gotten lax on my
daily practice. I am glad I always have a place to go back to

when I slip into bad habits. Just like the gym, it is hardest when you are getting started, and, even if you take a break, it is easier to return.

In 2021, I added guided breathwork coaching to my practice to help me with releasing stress and trauma. Having a structured process with a coach also provides me with a means of accountability. In an article about the rising popularity of breathwork, Mark Hyman, head of strategy and innovation at the Cleveland Clinic Center for Functional Medicine explains, "Breathwork has been shown to increase parasympathetic activity, heart rate variability, physiological flexibility, [and] is one of the greatest tools I have in my medical toolbox to help individuals manage stress, [which] has become an epidemic in our society."[2] Some of my most creative breakthroughs have occurred after a breathwork session after weeks of feeling blocked.

WEEK 4: IDENTIFY A UNICORN SPACE

In Eve Rodsky's 2022 book, *Finding your Unicorn Space*, she recommends that "finding creativity in a too busy world is an amazing resource for rediscovering the parts of you that may have taken a backseat as your responsibilities in life have piled on." When I started reading Eve's book, I found a good place to start was looking back to my childhood and remembering things that brought me joy.

Music, dance, art, writing, or returning to a dormant sport or hobby are all places that can be a source of unicorn space. You will negotiate dedicated time for that activity on a weekly basis so that you can immerse yourself in something that reminds you of who you are and that helps charge your batteries for the challenges of the week ahead. This is the antidote to exhaustion, doom scrolling, and Netflix binging. It is life-giving and only exists to remind you that joy and creative expression are part of your life's journey. It is where you feel free.

As someone with a chronic illness, I have had to evolve my unicorn space over the years. Initially, it was figure skating. In my twenties, it evolved to downhill skiing and Zumba dance. Eve's book encouraged me to dig deep and figure out what I could do today just for the sheer pleasure of it, which led me to start writing this book.

Month 2: Dream

Month 2 is about exploration and creativity. How can you turn your passions into a career? Is that working for someone else or exploring your entrepreneurial leadership? What are you doing when you get lost in a flow state and lose track of time?

WEEK 5: REFLECT ON YOUR ENERGY LOG.

Review your list of what energizes and drains you. Here are some questions to reflect on:

- What in your day that drains you can you minimize?
- Can you outsource mundane tasks or partner with other people in your community to share the load (carpool, babysitting, etc.)?

- Can you ask family and friends for more help?

- Are there some tasks you are taking on at work that are invisible labor and not energizing to you? Can you bring someone on to take them over for you?

- Remember, every yes you say to the world is a no you say to your time to recharge yourself.

After reviewing my own reflections, I leaned on family for more support with dinner meal prep (my dad is a great cook!) and carpool for driving the kids to and from their many after-school activities. I also requested that my husband take over the dishes, and I now buy my groceries online for curbside pickup to reduce the amount of time it takes.

WEEK 6: IDENTIFY YOUR VALUES

When you get closer to your unique mission that is aligned with your values, your momentum goes from feeling like you are pushing a rock uphill to letting one roll downhill unimpeded. Once you identify and prioritize your personal values, you can identify a dream life that is uniquely aligned to you. We were all raised with the expectations and dreams of prior generations placed on us. It is important to recognize that what served you in your teens and twenties may not be what is serving you now.

Taproot provides a wonderful values activity to narrow down your own.[3]

Determine your core values

From the list below, choose and write down every core value
that resonates with you. Do not overthink your selection. As
you read through the list, simply write down the words that feel
like a core value to you personally. If you think of a value you
possess that is not on the list, write it down.

Abundance	Curiosity	Inspiration	Relationships
Acceptance	Daring	Intelligence	Reliability
Accountability	Decisiveness	Intuition	Resilience
Achievement	Dedication	Joy	Resourcefulness
Adventure	Dependability	Kindness	Responsibility
Advocacy	Diversity	Knowledge	Responsiveness
Ambition	Empathy	Leadership	Risk-Taking
Appreciation	Encouragement	Learning	Safety
Attractiveness	Enthusiasm	Love	Security
Autonomy	Ethics	Loyalty	Self-Control
Balance	Excellence	Making a Difference	Selflessness
Being the Best	Expressiveness	Mindfulness	Service
Benevolence	Fairness	Motivation	Simplicity
Boldness	Family	Optimism	Spirituality
Brilliance	Flexibility	Open-Mindedness	Stability
Calmness	Friendships	Originality	Success
Caring	Freedom	Passion	Teamwork
Challenge	Fun	Performance	Thankfulness
Charity	Generosity	Personal Development	Thoughtfulness
Cheerfulness	Grace	Peace	Traditionalism
Cleverness	Growth	Perfection	Trustworthiness
Collaboration	Happiness	Playfulness	Understanding
Community	Health	Popularity	Uniqueness
Commitment	Honesty	Power	Usefulness
Compassion	Humility	Preparedness	Versatility
Consistency	Humor	Proactivity	Vision
Contribution	Inclusiveness	Professionalism	Warmth
Cooperation	Independence	Punctuality	Wealth
Creativity	Individuality	Quality	Well-Being
Credibility	Innovation	Recognition	Wisdom
			Zeal

Group similar values together

Group them in a way that makes sense to you, personally. Create a maximum of five groupings. If you have more than five groupings, drop the least important groupings. See the example below.

Abundance	Acceptance	Appreciation	Balance	Cheerfulness
Growth	Compassion	Encouragement	Health	Fun
Wealth	Inclusiveness	Thankfulness	Personal Development	Happiness
Security	Intuition	Thoughtfulness	Spirituality	Humor
Freedom	Kindness	Mindfulness	Well-being	Inspiration
Independence	Love			Joy
Flexibility	Making a Difference			Optimism
Peace	Open-Mindedness			Playfulness
	Trustworthiness			
	Relationships			

Label the groups

Choose one word within each group that represents the label for the entire group. Again, do not overthink your labels. There are no right or wrong answers. You are defining the answer that is right for you. See the example below. The label chosen for the grouping is in bold.

Abundance	Acceptance	Appreciation	Balance	Cheerfulness
Growth	Compassion	Encouragement	Health	Fun
Wealth	Inclusiveness	Thankfulness	Personal Development	**Happiness**
Security	Intuition	Thoughtfulness	Spirituality	Humor
Freedom	Kindness	**Mindfulness**	**Well-being**	Inspiration
Independence	Love			Joy
Flexibility	**Making a Difference**			Optimism
Peace	Open-Mindedness			Playfulness
	Trustworthiness			
	Relationships			

Add a verb

Add a verb to each value label. Upon completion of my own values assessment, the terms *influence, innovation,* and *advocacy* were my strongest themes. This helped me understand why some roles that did not tie to a mission beyond making money were not interesting to me in the long term.

I added the verb *better,* as in I wanted to better people's situations, not make them worse. I grew up a lot in the following couple of years and lost my naive belief that if you work hard and stay positive you will automatically succeed in your career. I also learned that taking on a role that was out of alignment with my values left me restless and frustrated much of the time. By focusing on whether a decision helps me make things better, I can check in with my motivations.

WEEK 7: NETWORK

Now is a great time to reflect on people who spend the majority of their time aligned with what you have identified as your values. Who do you admire? Who always makes you feel good when you interact with them? It is time to ask for thirty minutes of their time to better understand how they found their own flow. What does that career day look like? How do they establish and hold boundaries in order to stay focused on their mission? What tools do they leverage to get back on track when life throws them a curveball? This step will accomplish a few things:

- You will reconnect with colleagues and friends from over the years. They may know of an opportunity you would want to consider.

- It will help you notice that no one gets a solution that stays perfect forever. Learning tools from others on how to "dance in the rain" is a lifelong process; no need to reinvent the wheel.

- The antidote to shame and hopelessness is connection. The easiest way to help yourself get unstuck is to be vulnerable with people who have earned the right to know you.

Make sure to ask for introductions to people in their networks that may be someone you would benefit from knowing. It is also a good practice for strengthening relationships to ask if there is anything you can do to be of service to them in return for taking the time to help you. If their suggestion is something you feel comfortable doing, make sure to follow through.

My friend Emma was at a crossroads in 2022. She had already been a successful tech CEO for ten years before starting her family. She knew she was ready to return to work when her baby turned nine months old. She had only worked for herself and wanted to gain more experience at a larger company, but any job had to work with the new demands of her life.

I introduced her to a few of my connections, including the CEO of a fast-growing startup and a director for a major sports brand. She ended up being offered an advisory role to the CEO at the startup, but they did not have the budget to bring her on full time. The sports brand loved her leadership and skillset but did not have the right role available. That senior director, though, introduced her to someone on a trust and safety team for a rental platform company with an available role. The manager at the rental platform company liked her so much that, when he moved to a new company to build out their team a week after her informational interview, he made her an offer to join him.

WEEK 8: CREATE A PERSONAL AND PROFESSIONAL MISSION STATEMENT

The mission statement helps you clarify and align your personal and professional mission, via a mantra (or catchphrase) that's easy to communicate and keep top of mind. Once you have your mission statement, you can prioritize your existing and potential opportunities, skill development, and outreach according to how well they match your personal and professional reason for being.

To create your mission statement, ask yourself the following questions:

- What do you love?
- What are you good at?
- What does the world need?
- What will they pay you for?

Here is an example from my own brainstorming. I love advocating for marginalized women and children. I am good at directing resources (time, money, and focus) for innovation towards nontraditional areas. The world needs more diversity in product design and more women leaders.

To be able to use these mission statements to uncover and evaluate unexpected opportunities, start with answering the question "who do I want to be when I grow up?" Some exercises you can use to help your creativity along include the following:

- Review LinkedIn and identify people you admire.
- Identify ten people whose job is similar to one you'd love to have.
- Reach out to schedule networking calls and informational interviews.

During my own journey, I connected with old colleagues and strangers. I spoke with organizations ranging from startups, nonprofits, and for-profit companies in a range of industries including automation controls, cybersecurity, technology, and

> "I realized that my genius is less about schooling and certifi-
> cations and trainings, and more about my natural gifts—the
> things that I would never need to go to school to 'learn.'
> When I pivoted to doubling down on those things, and shin-
> ing that light more brightly, I could see opportunities more
> clearly and several opportunities found me."
>
> **—Tiana**

social work. I used my personal mission statement to evaluate if
those roles aligned with the direction I wanted to grow.

My mission statements are as follows:

- Personal: To relentlessly advocate for marginalized people's
  right to mental and physical health in order to thrive.

- Professional: To bring influential leaders and innovation
  together to address social justice issues at scale.

Month 3: Plan

Working in the semiconductor industry, I learned a lot about
the properties of silicon. No processor we shipped was sent
without a very specific set of instructions on how long you
could run it, at what temperature range, and what you could
expect. Now that isn't to say that it would not perform outside
that range, but we could not guarantee the advertised results if
you let it overheat, let it run too long, or tried to use it in a cor-
rosive environment. It always seemed ironic to me that we put
more time into establishing guidelines for how to use and not
abuse processors for work, but there was no spec sheet for people. Month 3 is about creating your own personal spec sheet.

WEEK 9: LIFESTYLE GOALS

Every phase of your life will bring different constraints and opportunities for career advancement. It is important to understand the major dials of your life in the areas of travel, relocation, flexibility, upward mobility, and skill enhancement when starting to plan for the future. When you can identify what you want your life to look like and marry that with your "why," you can start to plan for the right next step. This week, complete the following inventory for where you are today:

Travel

Define the percentage of travel you can accommodate, given your life responsibilities inside and outside of work. Be clear with yourself and others what your maximum travel capabilities are. Remember to revisit this every couple of years, because it will vary based on evolving education, caretaking, and life responsibilities.

Relocation

Are you open to moving at this time? Some stages of life offer more mobility than others. Many opportunities to climb the ladder in corporate America require frequent relocation. Be realistic with yourself about whether this works for your stage of life.

Skills

Identify what your dream job is in five years. Research what skills a strong candidate would need to shine in an interview for that role. Do an inventory of your current skills against that position and identify which skills you would need to add to position you well for the future you want. Use that information to identify your next role as one that can help fill those gaps.

Upward mobility

Identify companies that may be a good cultural fit for your needs and look on LinkedIn to see who you know that works there. Then, speak with employees at potential target employers to better understand their work culture. Ask clarifying questions about how they determine qualifications for follow-on roles at the company—for example, whether there are grade level gates—and ask them for any advice on what to negotiate for during your hiring to set you up for upward mobility.

When I was in my twenties, I was energized and excited by relocation and travel, and I moved from the Midwest to California and took a job that took me to thirty-six different countries. I focused on expanding my skills and worked in the areas of human resources, IT, marketing, supply chain, and sales, which built on my college experience in engineering. In my thirties, with a husband and young children, I locked my travel dial to less than 25 percent of the time, I opted out of opportunities that required relocation, and I focused on building C-suite and AI skills. In my forties, I am still locking my travel at less than 25 percent, but now I'm focusing on using the skills I enjoy as a keynote speaker, consultant, and author. I will no longer consider a job just because of the title and paycheck if the role is not aligned with the skills and mobility I am looking to build in this season of my career. I am looking forward to what my fifties will hold when my ability to relocate or travel will increase as I become an empty nester.

WEEK 10: INFORMATIONAL INTERVIEWING

Focus on scheduling informational interviews with the people you were introduced to from your networking in the seventh week of the plan (Month 2, Week 3). Gain clarity from them on what they like about the culture of their current employer and what they don't. Understand the expectations for work outside of business hours and how flexible they are to accommodate people with responsibilities outside of work. Ask them if they know anyone who is hiring for people with your skill set. If they say yes, ask for an introduction. Target two informational interviews a week until you secure your next role.

LinkedIn is a great tool for identifying new people that your connections may know, and most people are open to calls to help others grow in their career. During my informational interviews, I asked about how people got where they are today and shared my personal and professional mission statements as an ice breaker. Come with curiosity and a goal to build commonality. People like to help people that they see potential in.

I have gotten clients, jobs, and funding using this method. When I was ready to sell my AI software company, I was even able to find someone interested in buying it using this method. When the lawyers at Apple notified my cofounder that we were building "potentially competing technology to something they may build in the future" and offered him a team and a $12 million budget to bring our work in-house, I felt defeated. I turned to LinkedIn to find a home for myself and our Android roadmap. By scheduling time with CEOs in the trust and safety for children space, I was able to identify an opportunity for an acqui-hire with a larger player in the market, and also to continue the work we had started to enhance their product offering. It was a win–win situation that I could not have crafted without connecting and learning where they were in their journey and how I might be able to accelerate their goals.

When you come with a service mindset and a focus on finding win–win solutions, you will find the people who want to be alongside you on your growth journey. Don't be surprised if they start to believe in you more than you do in yourself!

> "Instead of asking yourself 'What if it doesn't work?' ask yourself 'But what if it does?'"
> —Kristin

WEEK 11: DON'T ACCEPT THE FIRST OFFER

Explore upward mobility and expectations as you narrow down your opportunities. Ask people that you network with at the company things they wish they had asked for when negotiating their new role (vacation time, grade level, pay, stock options, etc.). I have seen senior leaders come into organizations at too junior of a level, expecting to be able to move around once they got inside. Many companies will only allow employees to apply for jobs that are one or two levels above where they are today, and it can lead to a frustrating experience once they have been there for a year or two and are looking to grow. Finding a role with the right balance of travel, flexibility, growth, and culture should be your focus.

Although it can feel really uncomfortable to ask questions about money and perks, it is critical to better understand the landscape you are entering in order to negotiate a more favorable employment contract. It is well documented that men tend to ask for more when job hunting, and this can have a cumulative impact on the financial health of families—in the hundreds of thousands of dollars over decades. According to an article in *bizwomen*, "By not negotiating a starting salary, an individual stands to lose more than $500,000 by age sixty, reports suggest. Men are more than four times as likely as women to negotiate their first salary."[4]

Timing is important for negotiation. I recommend waiting until you have an offer in hand before asking for more. Based on the research you do ahead of time, you will be able to determine whether you want to ask for more money, stock, time, or all of the above for your offer. I am not saying you will get everything you ask for, but no company is going to revoke an offer because you asked whether it was the best they can do. Remember, you are the candidate they want and have invested

"I made a change when the job I had was winding down and all the jobs I was looking at online didn't excite me. While I COULD do them, I didn't WANT to do them."

—Allison G.

lots of time and money into screening. Don't sell yourself short to get in the door, as this is the best time for managers to be able to get you a competitive salary, extra vacation time, a signing bonus, or more stock options. Once you are part of a company, there is a finite pool of incentives that need to be divided among teams, which makes those incentives a scarcer commodity. Begin with the end in mind, and secure a package that makes you feel valued and will keep you satisfied even if you don't get a raise next year!

My first major career transition into sales happened in my late twenties, when I was joining a new industry with an unproven skill set. I calculated what my current total compensation was and added 20 percent. I told the hiring manager that is what I needed to come over. The major problem with that was it was above the pay bands for the role. It took two weeks of very uncomfortable waiting for my updated offer to come back, but I was paid what I negotiated for and stayed in that role for five years. When I met the senior executives while onboarding with the company, I introduced myself, and they replied "I know who you are, I had to approve your hiring package. We feel you are worth the investment." I stayed in that role longer than any other because I felt valued, and it was worth the discomfort of not settling.

WEEK 12: PERSISTENCE

Wash, rinse, and repeat until you have an offer in hand or you have clearly defined a company you want to launch. This networking by informational interview effort may take weeks,

> "When in doubt, act. You can make another decision tomorrow."
>
> **—Lisa**

months, or even years. But with every conversation, you are building your external brand, getting clarity for yourself on what you want for the next five years, and finding a culture that aligns with your lifestyle needs and values. No conversation is ever wasted, and always remember that finding out what you don't want is just as valuable as finding what you do want.

I have reinvented my career from engineer to sales director to AI evangelist to CEO to consultant to keynote speaker and now to author. This is a framework and process you can revisit when that familiar restless feeling starts to creep in and tells you it is time for a new adventure in your career. It is time to think of your career path as a portfolio of experiences as opposed to a straight line to retirement with a pension.

NAVIGATING FORWARD

- Start slowly, and integrate more wellness practices into your life. Set a goal date to start your bigger change, and select the wellness practices that appeal to you to help you prepare for that date.

- If you feel stuck in a toxic environment, remember that you have to get out of that system before you can start to heal from the effects it is having on you. Consider a medical leave, if it is available, to work on your burnout without setback triggers.

- Your career reboot can be as fast as ninety days or as long as a couple of years.

- This is a process you can revisit when you are sensing burnout, boredom, or a lack of psychological safety creeping into your daily life.

- No time is ever wasted when it is used for slowing down to tune into your own wisdom, networking to build your community of supporters, and visualizing what success looks like on your own terms. Even if you decide to stay in your current situation, there will be adjustments and boundaries you define that will increase your satisfaction.

PART 4

Many Ways to Go

CHAPTER 12

Smashing Success

"Your spark is the unique essence that burns bright
within you. Your spark makes you YOU."

—Sally Clarke

Leadership evolves through the seasons of your life. When you are building your skills and your network, it can feel like a mountain hike in the summer. There is excitement all along the journey: wildlife to spot, lakes to discover, and flowers in bloom. Although you are fighting gravity up the mountain, you are energized and inspired to forge ahead for the simple pleasure of it. The goal of reaching the summit is more than enough to offset any discomfort you may feel along the way.

Over time, you notice the beauty of a season change into fall, but the journey view is evolving into a colorful display of fall leaves and milder temperatures. You are close enough to the summit that it is easier to keep going then turn back around for a break. You have learned your pace and are continuing to build your endurance. Although you may be moving a little

"I started connecting with female founders and entrepreneurs over LinkedIn to build out my community. I connected
with so many amazing women that I decided to start my
podcast, The Empower Podcast, to interview other women
leaders on their entrepreneurial journeys. It was such an
encouragement to me through difficult times."

—Emily

slower, you are making just as much progress, as you are better
at wayfinding and knowing your own limits.

Just when it seems you have this whole process figured out,
winter sets in. As the temperatures drop and the trail gets covered
with snow and ice, there are unforeseen obstacles to your journey. You are looking for a well-paved path to make your climb
more tenable. Some days, it feels like you take one step forward,
two steps back, and it can be tempting to turn around and give
up when the peak is in sight. After all, you have been working
against gravity for many years, if not decades, now, and your
reserves are depleted. It seems crazy to quit, since you invested
so much into reaching this summit, but you start to wonder if
you even climbed the right mountain. This is when burnout is
at its highest.

The good news about all of these moments is that spring is
just around the corner. It will be a time for the ground to thaw
and new life to grow. You can take in the view from higher
ground and be inspired again for where your journey will take
you next. You notice that some of your path onward is going to
be aided by gravity, and you have all new vistas to explore. You

know that life will never be all downhill, but you can enjoy the support you feel with each step as the ground rises to meet you.

This is what it feels like when you have found your mission-aligned career focus. You no longer need to cling to the well-worn paths but can follow your own curiosity and intuition by noticing what energizes you. You find the people you want to take the journey with, and you let yourself be fully seen. It is a place of abundance and opportunity, no longer hampered by the fear of scarcity during the winter. The seasons will always cycle, but don't forget: You now know that, when the winter comes, it is only a season. There will be new vistas to climb come spring, and it's okay to rest and recharge.

Once you have gotten clear on your personal mission and vision, it is time to find your tribe. This can be at a corporation, a small business, or your own startup. The goal is to find a group of people with diverse talents that are energized to solve some of the same challenges you are. Gaining clarity, not only on the problem you want to solve but on what industry you want to focus on, will be helpful in finding your people.

I will use my company as an example. Minor Guard was focused on social justice. Our mission was to make kids safer online and in real life. In order to accomplish this mission, I needed cofounders with product management and data science experience to complement my skills in sales, marketing, and leadership. When we got past defining a vision for our minimum viable product, we realized that we had to focus on the K–12 education system in order to beta test our product. We needed to test our product on children, and in 2018, there was no cost-effective and reliable way to determine age with artificial intelligence. By focusing on a pilot within the education system, we could ground-truth one variable for our solution, which was that the person using the product was under eighteen. The second challenge we had was that all social media apps had an embedded camera in them. The data was end-to-end encrypted, so this was also addressed because school computers only use the native camera on the device.

Then the big issue got clear from this discovery: We had no one on our team with experience or a network to sell to education customers. Given that we were not only trying to harness cutting-edge technology but working on sensitive, regulated data, we needed someone with access who was a trusted advisor to our potential buyer—school CTOs. This helped us to realize that bringing in this expertise was critical to our success, so we recruited a board of directors member who brought this experience and network into our company. By building an advisory board to help on the technical challenges that were engineered around, including AI leaders from Apple, Microsoft, Google, and Intel, we were able to scale our technology roadmap into major players in the technology industry, leveraging cutting-edge artificial intelligence capabilities.

Today, I advise early-stage companies on how to grow revenue, leverage technology innovation, and raise capital in order to translate the best ideas into products. It is such an honor to be able to align with primarily traditionally underrepresented operators to help them make their vision a reality. In order to succeed in the pressure cooker as an innovator, I suggest the following call to action:

1. Find your mission

2. Build a personal board of advisors

3. Identify an executive sponsor

This method of understanding your team's core skills and network can be applied to any environment, including the place you work today. The key to leading from any seat is to create a vision that inspires people to follow you. Working within a company, you will likely find many talented people who are not energized by the mission of their day jobs and are looking for something to work on in their nights and weekends that fills their soul. By defining a problem you want to address, you are able to galvanize talent at little to no cost in order to help them gain more satisfaction in their lives.

This was demonstrated for me time and time again during my eighteen years working in corporate America. When I was exploring this problem area in my early days of understanding the underlying technology and why the problem was scaling so fast, I leveraged personal and professional networks of loose connections to learn more. This process of informational interviews with experts was very intimidating; however, I have found that, when you approach people with a genuine interest to learn more about them and what they are great at, they really light up.

My interview tour brought me into contact with data scientists, physicians, entrepreneurs, nonprofit leaders, and the C-suite of the company I had worked at for ten years. It expanded my network of people invested not only in my company but in my journey, and that personal board of advisors has stayed with me years later as my focus has evolved to an even bigger mission. There were many times when I was intimidated to pick up the phone or ask for a meeting, but I realized that we are all hardwired to connect and looking for ways to use our power for something meaningful. When you can connect with people beyond their title and LinkedIn profile, you can build something well beyond your wildest dreams—inside your company or on your own.

NAVIGATING FORWARD

- Nothing good lasts forever, but nothing bad does either. If you are struggling for hope in your current situation there is a brighter future for you ahead.

- Success is a team sport; no one wins alone. Build your personal board of advisors to support you along the journey.

CHAPTER 13

Build for Your Mission with Intrapreneurship

"Balance is the epiphany that you don't have to be
everything to everyone all of the time."
—Vanessa Autrey

So you have identified your values and business mission statement. How do you go from ideation to a new role in your organization? The first thing to remember is that if your mission statement is not aligned with developing a product or service that can be monetized, you are creating a hobby, not a role. Looking for a volunteer organization that can leverage your expertise with a mission that aligns with your values is a great way to contribute without having to quit your day job or raise funds. If you think spearheading an initiative is the right path, below is a guide for how to methodically work toward your vision.

The first step in intrapreneurship is identifying the strategic alignment with your target organization's mission. If it is a large, publicly traded company, the annual report is a good place to start for a better understanding of their top-line goal for the coming year. It is important to align your value proposition with that goal. In addition, if you are currently employed there, quarterly update meetings with the top-level executives are a rich source of information for how you can help the company to grow revenue in alignment with your mission.

Focusing on ways to explore innovation by leveraging data from the public sector can be a great place to start. Many of the digital transformation and data challenges facing nonprofits, enterprise, and government are similar in nature: data privacy, cloud computing, artificial intelligence, and analytics. Key learnings and case studies are transferable assets and valuable to many companies' marketing and sales organizations to increase top-line revenue.

Most companies operate under a zero-based budget model, where to add funding for new work, they have to replace a priority from the prior year's budget. In order to help with prioritization, it is important to show how focusing the organization's resources on this new area would yield a better return on investment than current priorities. Identifying ways to cut costs, grow sales, or accelerate new markets can all be quantified in a ROI calculation, which will help align stakeholders on why they should stop doing something else in order to implement your vision. When you can speak to the finance, marketing,

> "Listen to your instincts. Those alarm bells going off are a sign that things need to change. And don't ever tell yourself that you don't have other options. You always have options. You may not like the options you have, but you always have options."
>
> **—Visa**

product, and sales leadership about how you will help them accomplish their goals, it is easier to align support. You can then create a role for yourself that allows you to shine and help grow the business at the same time.

The second step to launching an initiative within a company is establishing an executive sponsor. This is someone who has the ability to create and allocate budgets for projects, typically at the vice president level or higher. You need to be able to: quantify the return-on-investment opportunity for the role; demonstrate its tie to the strategic mission of the company; be able to explain the ecosystem for the players addressing the issue; and create a budgetary estimate (headcount and expense dollars). You would also need to do a proof of concept to test the idea. This may include travel dollars to meet with potential partners, time for job shadowing at the organization, hardware or software costs, and marketing support for a pitch deck.

Once you have this pitch deck in hand, it is important to map the key stakeholders across the company that could serve on your advisor board to help support the initiative. Your executive sponsor will be an invaluable resource to help you map stakeholders, and they will likely participate in setting up meetings with those key stakeholders to gain their buy-in. It is helpful to use free tools intended for entrepreneurs such as the Lean Canvas model or a business plan to help you identify the financial opportunity, target market, and resources required to execute the vision. This structured process will help you to have the correct data to create stakeholder buy-in beyond your executive sponsor, so if they transition on to a new role, you have others invested in your success. This will also create a pipeline of people who are available to help you resource a series A funding round, once you have taken your learnings from your minimum viable product and are ready to apply it to a more scalable solution.

BUILDING EXTERNAL PARTNERSHIPS

Partnerships are part art and part science. External organizations have numerous competing priorities (some of which are tied to contractually binding grants), so it can be challenging to gain mindshare for a project that does not help them directly with a top priority for the organization. Whether you partner with a for-profit or a 501(c)(3), finding the right organization to align with is key. It must be a mutually beneficial relationship and typically involves both monetary and technical support.

It is important to research any organization with which you want to cultivate a long-term relationship. I recommend volunteering for your target organization, watching documentaries about the topic, and listening to podcasts about it. It is important to be customer-focused in this relationship and to recognize that, at the end of the day, you are selling your company's capabilities to them, not doing a good deed. Even if you don't plan to charge for your services, it costs the organization time and allocation of internal resources to absorb new technology. Ask yourself whether this project is capable of self-sustaining after it deploys. If not, it is not a good fit.

It is important to work with a partner that is mission-aligned and ready to innovate. As with many public sector opportunities, expect things to move at a slow and steady pace. The collaboration will need to be reviewed at an executive and board level to proceed, and that takes time.

Once you have identified a partner, it is important to get a memorandum of understanding in place to ensure you are both aligned on the scope of the partnership. The more explicit you can be about what is and is not included in the project, the better, including timelines. This gives both organizations an opportunity to ensure a mutual understanding of scope and timing so that there are no surprises. Bad news is okay, but surprises are damaging to a relationship. I encourage overcommunication where possible and assigning a project manager to oversee the project. I also recommend quarterly executive syncs to ensure that all key stakeholders stay engaged with the project and that the working-level team has an opportunity to share their progress and successes with leadership.

> "You are your own best advocate. If someone is not giving you the opportunity, make the opportunity for yourself. Don't ever stop putting yourself out there, and do not stop chasing your dreams. You are enough."
>
> —Sara

SETTING OUT ON YOUR OWN

There may come a time where your idea and the company's
goals are no longer aligned. This is a great time to explore doing
a startup. There is a wealth of information on the startup journey across podcasts, books, and conferences to help you explore
this path. I found the *StartUp* podcast from Gimlet Media and
Masters of Scale from Reed Hoffman very educational about
what to expect and how to grow your business. *The Lean Startup*
by Eric Rese presents a wealth of knowledge on how to avoid
typical mistakes new founders make.

As discussed in previous chapters, I recommend finding a
cofounder whose skills are different from yours. Although it is
tempting to go into business with someone who thinks just like
you, it is much better for innovation to have someone who com-
plements your strengths and provides a diversity of thought. It
is also important to surround yourself with mentors who are
experienced in startups to guide you through the process. Many
communities fund free Small Business Association classes to
help founders along in all areas of running a business, including
incorporating, marketing, accounting, legal, IT, HR, etc.

SOLID ADVICE

Kelly Solid is a general manager who uses his business development skills in sales, negotiation, enterprise software, and
strategic partnerships to help law enforcement build cases using
analytics to catch sex traffickers. He offered me some great
advice on how to get started.

Start with what you know

Kelly worked for the past twelve years supporting law enforcement at the federal, state, and local levels in the area of investigative analytics. He wondered whether this experience could be applied to the problem of sex trafficking. He was working for Securus Technologies, a US company driving efforts to better serve the incarcerated through rehabilitative justice. How could he use this vast amount of data and its investigative tools to assist law enforcement? Would his company even be open to using resources to tackle this problem with no intent for profit?

Securus was uniquely positioned with a customer base that intersected more than 80 percent of the cities where sex trafficking was most prolific—Atlanta, Dallas, New York, Miami, New Orleans, Portland, San Diego, and Seattle, to name a few. Enlightened with this information, Kelly needed to fully understand the intersect between corrections and sex trafficking.

Start with who you know

After receiving the blessing from his management to pursue this initiative, Kelly was back to: "Where do I start?" Well, he started with who he knew—his network of men and women in law enforcement that he had developed over the years.

One such contact, a mover and shaker in the Northern California law enforcement community, told him that he lacked experience in trafficking, but he could introduce Kelly to me so we could discuss ideas on where to start.

I shared my passion for using technology to fight sex trafficking with Kelly, and guided him to a smart and focused businesswoman, Emily Kennedy, to look for further possible synergies.

Emily was a founder and CEO at Marinus Analytics, which developed Traffic Jam, an artificial intelligence product designed to identify sex trafficking in the hundreds of thousands of online sex ads. Emily, in turn, introduced Kelly to one of her company's partners at the time, DeliverFund, a nonprofit with the mission to "cut the head off the snake." They wanted to assist law enforcement in identifying, arresting, and prosecuting traffickers through the use of investigative analytics.

And that's what Kelly is good at—investigative analytics. He had found a possible home for how Securus could assist on the front lines in the fight against sex trafficking in the US. Securus found a considerable intersection between corrections and sex trafficking, and they continue to explore ways to work with law enforcement and great organizations like DeliverFund and Marinus Analytics in their fight against crime.

Like Kelly Solid, you can lead from where you are. You can affect change at your company, community, or religious organization today. Look for problems that technology can help with. Tie it back to places where it costs money to the organization (lawsuits, time, or resources; it is always good to think about what keeps the CFO up at night). Build a team around you to help you ideate and prototype small minimum viable products so you can fail fast and learn. This will help you home in on the great idea that is worth pitching to your leadership team or investors.

NAVIGATING FORWARD

- Quitting your job may not be the right move at this time. There are many ways to add meaning to your career though volunteering, coaching, and mentoring.

- When advocating for new ways of approaching work, it is important to create the connection between your project idea and the goals for the company. If you can show data to support that the return on investment for your project outweighs something already on your plate, you can lobby to prioritize this project over the other.

- It is crucial to build a network to support your goals. This can start inside your organization, but you'll likely need outside help as well.

CHAPTER 14

Spark Passion with Entrepreneurship

"It takes twenty years to build a reputation and five minutes to ruin it. If you think about that, you'll do things differently."

—attributed to Warren Buffett

According to a 2020 survey from *Forbes*, 61 percent of women surveyed were planning a major career change after the pandemic. In addition, one in four women surveyed are interested in starting their own business.[1] Emily Kennedy and I are successful startup executives who have built our social impact businesses from scratch. We have released an Entrepreneurship 101 series e-course to help accelerate women toward success. In our course, titled Spark Passion, we demystify the process of founding a company and provide free resources to help launch your business, find your customers, build your minimum viable product, and prevent burnout with community and wellness practices. We have partnered with Women in Data to create coaching and community for women founders across the globe.

I spent 2019 rebuilding my career. After leaving my CEO position with Minor Guard, I took a position as VP in the acqui-hire company. A little over a year later, I was surprised to be let go from that position. The following week, I was scheduled to give a keynote address about my career "success" for the 2020 Women on Boards event at the California capital. Talk about feeling like a fraud. Over the next few months, I felt lost and adrift as I was having to redesign my career yet again, but this time with much more experience.

I have always been drawn to a challenge and enjoy turning an idea into reality. I spent the early part of my career in corporate America, where I was the most satisfied when I could come into a situation that was not functioning well and could bring in the vision and execution to improve the situation quickly. I also learned that once something was functioning well, I was bored and wanted to move on to the next challenge. This makes entrepreneurship and consulting a good fit.

I entered the software startup world to address a very specific issue: children creating and distributing illegal images on their phones. In order to identify this material and block it from being saved on the device, we had to train an artificial intelligence model to recognize nudity. I will never forget the call I received my first month as CEO from my CTO, sharing that they needed millions of "hot dog" photos to train our models. Apparently, it is not hard to find millions of labeled pictures of naked women, but men were a bit more challenging. I am grateful that a friend turned me on to a website that had what we needed, so I could share that instead of having to go find it all myself!

Launching a business from the ground up was the best way to accelerate. Overnight, I went from an engineering and sales leader to head of marketing, IT, legal, HR, and janitorial services. Because I was bootstrapping the business with my cofounder, we were trying to be as frugal as possible. I did not have a computer of my own, so he gave me an extra one he had, a Mac. I have been a lifelong PC user, and this change set me back to first-grade levels of proficiency doing email and presentations for the following six months. That "free" computer cost me more frustration and velocity than anything. If I could do that over, I would. If you bet on yourself, invest in yourself for what you need to come out of the gates swinging.

When it is your company, there are no more uninterrupted vacations or weekends until you have an exit. It is important to make sure you are spending your one life on those areas that energize you. Only you can know what lifts your energy and what drains it. In order to gain that clarity and prioritize what you will take on, I find the following considerations helpful:

Clarity of vision

In order to lead, it is important to know your "why" and make that transparent to your team. Your company culture should be aligned with that purpose. Integrity in how you operate will lead to long-term loyalty and growth for those who choose to join you on this crazy adventure of inventing the future.

"Listen to the market and what the market wants, even if that means creating something that doesn't exist yet. Selling something people want is the difference between success and failure for most companies."

—Mary

A relentless focus on the customer

Many founders fall in love with technology for technology's sake. They don't understand the need in the market or how to help potential customers become aware that they are addressing that pain point. There is much more to running a business than building cool stuff.

Building your company brand

Coming from large companies, I never had much of a need for a website, LinkedIn, or Twitter. I could lean on the brand of my employer to open doors. It is critical to ensure you own your pipeline and have regular touchpoints with your potential buyers to move them through the customer journey.

Wellness practices are not a luxury

The best day and the worst day as a founder are often spread out by hours and may happen a few times a day. You will need wellness practices in order to be effective for the long term. To recharge my batteries, I use meditation, walks, breathwork, and time with family and friends to recover from some of the harsh realities of an entrepreneurial life.

Done is better than perfect

If you are proud of your first product when you launched, you launched too late. It is important to get feedback from the market and keep iterating. You can't do that if you are keeping all your ideas hidden until they look Instagram perfect.

ACCESS TO CAPITAL

An article in *Forbes* claimed that only "two percent of venture capital investments go to companies solely founded by women, and 65 percent of firms still do not have a single female partner. If there is to be an increase in the success of diverse founders, there must first be a much larger increase in diversity at the capital allocator and partner level."[2] As a woman leader, your work is cut out for you. Despite whatever progress we've made, we still have a long way to go.

I have seen many incredible female leaders struggle to access the capital and sponsorship for success, especially women of color. Their companies are often much further along in product–market fit, and they are already achieving revenue goals, but the investors are not moving from conversations to checks for series A rounds. The implicit bias in access to capital needs to be compensated for so that the next founder of Bumble or Spanx doesn't give up before she disrupts her industry.

In order to learn how to build a fundable business, why not

partner with experienced founders who have run the funding gauntlet? You could try to figure it out on your own, spinning your wheels for months and staying in a job you don't love, but you could still end up months or years down the road in the same limbo, unsure of whether your idea to impact the world could have been viable. Sometimes, putting your dreams on hold is necessary, but in this time of uncertainty, wouldn't you much rather get clarity on your strategy so you can move forward? Instead, take a simple five weeks now to quickly validate your idea, so you can move forward confidently to change the world. It's not rocket science; it's about implementing proven strategies that can help you determine whether your passion can become a business that brings positive impact in the long term. An experienced partner can help you walk through the steps to gain momentum and have an actionable plan to move your idea forward.

When you can speak the language that investors understand about large untapped markets, scalable solutions, and fundable founding teams, you can free up the resources to make your dream a reality.

THE FOUNDER IS THE BRAND

Once you decide to launch a business, you become your new company's brand. It is important to select a platform to focus on for building an audience. I choose LinkedIn, because it is aligned best with the C-suite, board of directors, and entrepreneurship audience at which my message is targeted. I have been able to find talent for my company, raise funds, and explore mergers and acquisitions all via connections I have made on

> "The hardest part of being a founder is overcoming fear."
> —Sadie

LinkedIn. Do not underestimate the power of human connection (even virtually) to advance your mission and vision. When you are getting started here are some recommendations:

- Focus on building your connections. I had less than five hundred for the first five years. Now, I add a thousand per year.

- Post consistency matters. Set a weekly target for how many posts to do (my goal is one per day).

- Original content is important. Even if you are providing links to useful articles, videos, or blogs, write your own comments about them to show what your values and perspectives are.

Once you have started to find your rhythm with this process, I encourage you to leverage the media to help amplify your content. In order to be ready for this, make sure you have a professional-grade headshot ready and an executive bio. These will be requested from you each time you are selected for an article, keynote, or panel discussion. To get your reps in, I recommend the following:

- Set a goal of publishing an article or blog quarterly.

- Help a Reporter Out is a great free resource to apply to be published in magazines. You can also self-publish on LinkedIn.

- Sign up to participate with a curated thought leaders site. They will repost your material for free and have a good following from the C-suite globally. I use Thinkers360.

- Use no more than three hashtags per post, and include people or companies with large followings to help increase your visibility.

You will also want to leverage strategic networking at events. To make the most of this investment, I suggest identifying your target personas and the events they attend each year. Consider applying for a speaking slot rather than a booth. You build much more credibility that way and will avoid the large fees to attend the event. To be successful in applying, you will need the following:

- A bio, a topic list, and a syllabus
- A sizzle reel of your speaking engagements
- Testimonials from people who hire you

Panels and fireside chats are also a great way to build your credibility. Partnering with a moderator or interviewer can take some of the event-planning pressure off, and you can cocreate a compelling discussion in real time for the audience while establishing yourself as a subject matter expert.

Especially if you do not enjoy live public speaking, content creation is another useful avenue. This can take the form of blogs, podcasts, and social media posts. Never turn down an offer to be a guest on someone else's show. Having content that is professionally edited gives you more to work with in the future and helps you expand your network.

Blogs

Blogs should be around a thousand words on a topic. It is good for search engine optimization to include links to other websites in your article. Leverage buzzwords in the industry to make your article more discoverable, and tag those keywords in your article. Choose your image and headline carefully to create interest in your article.

Podcasting

Pick a theme that aligns with your brand identity; I choose to show the human side of tech. Know your target audience, and establish credibility with guests from your customers, authorities in the field, and C-suite leaders.

Social media

Pick one platform, and focus on getting good at that one. Leverage commercially available tools to help you schedule and automate your posts. Lately.ai is my favorite.

DISCOVERING YOUR CUSTOMERS

Gordon Moore's *Crossing the Chasm* is an excellent resource for learning how customers adopt new products and services for digital transformation. It is important to target the right customer profile in each vertical you're interested in. For example, if it is new software, look for the innovators. Find a beachhead customer who is tolerant of bugs to help you cocreate your product with the goal to have the customer need influence your product direction. (See the end of the chapter for a worksheet about finding your customer.) Nurture and develop relationships with people who will help you test your product over time.

Next, you need to identify your stakeholders, the champions and key decision-makers who will be part of the buying process for their company. Remember: Small wins bring big victories. Show people that you are differentiated through simple acts, such as reliability: When you say your product will do something, make sure it actually does.

These relationships take time to build. Start small and be consistent, and you can get the big wins. Have a service mindset: What can you do for each person you meet? Build a reputation as a giver, not a taker.

STEP INTO LEADERSHIP: CASE STUDY JENNIFER SAHA

Jennifer Saha found herself as many of us do: in a job we don't love, not making the money we'd like to. She asked her employer for what she thought she was worth, but she did not get the answer that she was hoping for. Rather than accepting a status quo that didn't provide the life she wanted, Jennifer decided to reboot her career. And she did this during the COVID-19 pandemic.

It was "super scary," she said. "And I had a bunch of personal life factors that compounded the amount of stress." She had been working for a national trade association for four years, and she had consistently taken on more responsibilities. She had

> "Building your own company is not always the solution
> when you need a change. You literally have to be obsessed
> with the problem you're trying to solve. Not your solution,
> the problem you are trying to solve. Because you may fail at
> the first iteration of that solution."
>
> **— Max**

been promoted for her great work, and she saw a bright future
with the company. "I really felt valued," she said.

A few years in, she got married and was trying to have a
baby. "We struggled with fertility issues," she said. "The company was super supportive. I'd had a bunch of miscarriages. I
needed time off, and, anything I needed, they were there for it."

She was feeling valued, supported, seen—all the things that
matter. She was killing it. She and her husband were finally able
to conceive, and she went on paid maternity leave. While she
was on leave, several of her peers were promoted and had been
given substantial raises. When she came back, she was no longer
level with her peers.

The feedback she received during leave was that her contribution was missed, that she was valuable. She also did some
research. Both her level of responsibilities and the revenue she
brought into the company were still more than those peers who
had been promoted during her absence. So she asked her supervisor to bring her back to parity with the people she was ostensibly
being measured against and to reduce her 80–90 percent travel to
something more manageable while she had a young child.

"I'd done my homework," Jennifer said. "I ran the numbers.
I knew exactly to the penny how much I was bringing in for this

organization. I even knew what my colleagues were bringing in. I was prepared."

But it wasn't the slam dunk she thought it would be. Her supervisor hesitated, then said, "Let me talk to the CEO, and I'll get back to you."

Eventually, the supervisor did get back to her. She called back while Jennifer was at lunch with her mother and aunt; they were meeting the baby for the first time. Jennifer said, "I have to take this call" and stepped outside.

"I've discussed it with the CEO," the supervisor said, "and we're not moving forward with that at this time." They were also resistant to reducing her travel to anything less than 50 percent of her work.

"It was just like I was shattered," Jennifer said. "My career has always been a very strong measure of my self-worth, and my career and my position are a large part of my personal identity. She already felt isolated, stuck home with a newborn all day, and she now felt that her company was saying, "You're not as good as those peers who bring measurably less to the organization."

"I wasn't angry," she said. "I accepted it." She internalized the implicit feedback: *You're not good enough.* "And so, I came home, and there were a lot of tears." The flexibility and support she had felt from the company had evaporated.

She spoke with her husband. "He's always been my partner in life and everything," she said. "So he, of course, is always team Jen. 'That's absolute bull,' he said. We agreed that this wasn't going to work." The job she had loved "quickly went from my forever dream job to 'I need to get the hell out of here.'"

The straw that broke the camel's back was not just that she

felt like she wasn't valued. She was being told that they wouldn't respect her boundaries either. Fifty percent travel, as you can imagine, would be extremely difficult with a toddler at home.

She started to look at her options. "I don't have another job. I can't quit. I've got to figure out what I want to do. And so I went and talked with a colleague and friend who worked at a national IT consulting firm. He had always said, 'I want to be one of your first calls if you are ever looking for something.'" This was a clever part of Jennifer's career reboot—to network before leaving her current position.

"So I said, 'I am looking! Let's have lunch.'"

Jennifer met with her friend, who was high up in a large company, and she told him the story.

"They are idiots," he said. "They're going to lose you, and they don't even know what they're losing."

He quickly pivoted. "We would hire you in a heartbeat—no questions asked—but there's still going to be some travel required with this job. I'm hearing you say that you don't want that."

Jennifer thought about it, then said, "Maybe once or twice a year, but not monthly even."

"Look," her friend continued, "why don't you start your own company? We will sign up and be your first clients."

"I was like, 'Okay, you're crazy. There's a ton of risk in that. I need income. I just had a baby.' But the more I thought about it, the more it seemed like a good idea. I ran some numbers: How many clients would I need to be able to make what I was earning at the previous job? And, luckily, my medical was covered through my husband's job. So I really only needed two, maybe three clients. *Wow*, I thought. *I feel like I could do that.*"

She discussed with her husband what it would mean financially, what it would mean for their marriage, for their responsibilities as parents, all of the important aspects of her life.

"He was like, 'Go for it.'"

It all made sense on paper, and the support of both her husband and a friend—and potential client—made it clear to Jennifer that starting her own business was realistic.

"I knew it would be a risk," she said, "but when we sort of sketched it out, the list of pros was way longer than the cons."

So she filed company corporation paperwork, got a website, bought the domain, had a logo designed, and she got the ball rolling. This was in the summer of 2019, and Jennifer was now the CEO of Golden Bridge Strategies, a business advisory and government consulting firm.

"I gave notice at my job," she said. "I had gone back only a month before, so they were surprised. I told them I would give them two months instead of two weeks." This extra notice would allow the company to transition more slowly, but it also let Jennifer get her ducks in a row.

She continued to network and was able to connect with another potential client. "I knew, starting off, that I was going to be okay."

But she was still working—and traveling—for her current employer. On a work trip, with her husband and baby in tow, she "was just feeling weird. I took a pregnancy test. Sure, I'm pregnant again, I have a five-month-old, I just gave notice at my job, I'm starting a consulting firm, and I'm pregnant. So I had a moment of *Oh, what have I done? I just threw away my solid income. How does maternity leave work when you are just a consultant and you have contract retainer clients?* All of these questions are freaking me out and swirling in my brain."

She knew she had her husband's support, and she trusted herself. She knew she'd figure it out. "The first few months, I was a little nervous, because when you start contracting with someone, you don't realize that you don't actually get money in my bank account right then. From the day someone says, 'Yeah, let's do business together, let's put you on monthly retainer, and you can be our consultant,' it's a solid three months until you ever see any money out of those clients. I didn't really factor all of that into my budget."

Despite the slow trickle of income, things were going well. "I have my clients, they all know I'm having a baby. We'll make it work; everything will be fine."

And then the pandemic hit. "I was having my baby the day that it was declared a pandemic in the United States," she said. This was March of 2020. "So there were a lot more questions: How is this going to impact my business? How is this going to impact my maternity leave? That's nonexistent now."

But she got through it. "The pandemic has been awful for so many people. But for a consulting business that focuses on government—one sector of the economy that was spending drastically more money than ever before—it was incredibly successful."

She hired her first employee in 2020, when she had five clients, and Golden Bridge has continued to grow. "Today, we are five full-time employees strong. We have eighteen clients on retainer with us—Fortune 500 companies. Our clients are happy." Those first two clients who gave her the support she needed to reboot are still working with her.

"I'm transitioning at this point into more of a business owner and a strategist as opposed to a day-to-day operator. And it's been a transition for me, for sure, but I've never been happier. I have never once looked back and said, 'Man, maybe I shouldn't have left that job.' I'm thankful that they doubted me. I'm thankful that they questioned my value, because it gave me the motivation to do this.

"I mean, you can draw the conclusions: I needed two clients to make my annual salary at the old company. And now I have eighteen clients. It was a very, very profitable decision. The financial freedom allows me to not be stressed about having another kid. But what's exciting about it to me is just that I'm able to do what I'm passionate about. You make your own decisions, you make your own calls, and having that freedom is incredible."

I can relate to Jen's experiences—leading my own company was the best street MBA I could get. I learned how to prioritize, assess risk, build my brand, establish a company culture, and create new products. It rounded me out well beyond my traditional career experience. The Small Business Association provides a lot of free courses needed for running a successful small business. Check out your local office for offerings in areas like HR, accounting, creating a business plan, and more. Make sure you start with clarity and capital but also the other resources that you need. Don't try to reinvent the wheel; leverage your network to go faster.

NAVIGATING FORWARD

- When you decide to bet on yourself, invest in the business tools you will need to be successful up front.

- Build your brand intentionally; as the founder, you are the company.

- If you are not focused on your customers to help you define your offering, you will build something that does not sell. You need to focus on solutions for large-market problems, not one-off issues.

HOW TO FIND YOUR CUSTOMER

Beta customers are not necessarily people that will buy your product. These are companies/people that like trying the latest and greatest products. They don't mind some glitches and are willing to provide feedback on how they would see the product being a better fit for their business. They are people that will talk about products and services they love and are ones that people go to for recommendations.

1. Who is in my network that would be a potential beta customer for my product?

   _____

   _____

2. What industries may benefit from my product? Select one that you want to focus on.

   _____

   _____

3. In business-to-business sales, often the people who would pay for your product are not the people who would use it directly. The people whose teams would benefit from your product need to be able to explain why the expense is justified. These people are your "champions" who help you navigate the decision makers (business, technical, service delivery) and advocate for your company during the decision-making process.

4. Which people/companies are you focused on selling to? Who in your network could introduce you to people there for discovery meetings?

    _____

    _____

5. Identify the types of people they will have to internally convince to pay to try your product. How would each of those roles benefit from saying yes to your product (estimate a $ benefit to them)?

    _____

    _____

   Business is conducted by people. Delivering on your commitments and having a service mindset are the bricks and mortar for building lasting relationships.

1. Who have you gone above and beyond for in your past business relationships? What is the unique value proposition you bring to a company/investor?

    _____

    _____

continued →

2.   What motivated you to select a teammate, partner, or
      vendor in the past? Did they do anything special that
      stood out to you?

      _____

      _____

      Building a business is a series of milestones, and it is a
long game. Building a business from the ground up requires
a broad set of skills that you may not have developed yet.
Partnership and advisory boards can be lifelines to fill in
gaps in your knowledge. Each city has a Small Business
Association that offers free courses to new business owners. Check out www.sba.gov for your local resources.

1.   What business skills are strengths you have (Operations,
      Finance, Sales, Marketing, HR, Legal, Product Develop-
      ment, IT)?

      _____

      _____

2.   What gaps do you have? What is your next step for
      learning or partnering to fill those gaps?

      _____

      _____

CHAPTER 15

Follow the Yellow Brick Road

"You've always had the power, my dear.
You just had to learn it yourself."

—Glenda the Good Witch, *The Wizard of Oz*

W hen I was in elementary school, there was lots of excitement to learn about space, as NASA was going to be launching the first teacher into orbit. I think many kids of my generation thought their teacher was special enough to get chosen, and I remember that mine applied. As we waited for the selection process to be completed that year, we would get updates and envision our teacher on a spaceship for months before anyone took off.

When the date finally came for us to watch the *Challenger* launch, we all huddled around a TV on the elementary school carpet to watch this moment in history that we felt a part of.

As we all participated in the countdown, it was a moment of glee. Then, it turned into a moment of horror when the ship exploded before our eyes.

I think this was when I developed an underlying fear of success. That moment stuck in my brain as a time to be careful what you wish for when it comes to career success. The 1980s was a time when girls were not only raised to believe they *could* be anything; we received a subtle message that we *should* be everything. We learned for the first time in school about women's role in history, and we were going to be the generation that was able to maximize our potential after our mothers had fought for equal rights.

I wrote this book for that little girl and the others like me that wanted to do something important but were also scared of success. That girl who got a D in spelling and grammar that year and decided she should focus on math and science because it was easier for her. I bet she would be amazed to know that she grew up to be a published author one day.

My health has steadily declined since my first pregnancy, when my immune system started attacking itself. Although I looked okay on the outside, I knew something had changed on the inside. I entered 2022 with my doctor telling me I did not look sick enough to have the serious disease I suspected I had. In February, I got a second opinion from an expert who diagnosed me within five minutes of reading my chart. This validated the gut feeling and confirmed that I wasn't just imagining all my symptoms.

When my daughter was six, I promised her at a mommy and daughter tea party that I would take her to the Eiffel Tower when she turned sixteen. With my health as it was, I was unsure I would be here to fulfill that promise, so I booked the trip for April of 2022, when she was eleven. To justify the travel, I would give the keynote at the World AI Cannes Festival, and we'd head to Paris after the talk.

On April 6th, I got a call from my doctor no one wants to get: "I am sorry, but we found some things on your CT scan we did not expect to see. You need a consult with a vascular surgeon immediately. You have an aneurysm, and we may need to do emergency surgery." For the next seventy-two hours, I got many tests and consults while trying to keep it together in front of my kids.

In the waiting time for the results, I decided that, whatever they told me, I was going to go on the trip. I wanted to keep my promise to my daughter. I was raised to believe that all you have is your word, and I did not want to go to the grave with a promise unkept. In the event that I died while we were abroad, I planned for my daughter to fly home with a CEO I advise and who has become a good friend of the years.

Twelve hours before my flight, my results came back. The aneurysm was small enough that it was safe to watch for now with repeat angiograms every six months until we decide to intervene surgically. A PET scan and an MRI showed no aneurysms in my brain, although my rheumatologist shared his concern I may be "littered" with them once my disease affected my vascular system. I had cancelled all the tours I booked, because I did not think we would be able to travel on our planned dates. But we got on a plane and shared special time touring the Louvre and seeing the Eiffel Tower together. I

Lee Christofferson

A promise kept: A special moment for me
and my daughter at the Eiffel Tower.

received a publishing contract the day my daughter and I
returned from our trip. I did not feel well enough to commit to
the project, so I decided to sit on it for a few months to see if I
would have the energy budget to write the book.

I spent the summer getting on the right medications to
manage my chronic disease. The first one made me suicidal, a
known side effect, so we had to go a more aggressive treatment
route. First, we needed to rule out bladder cancer to ensure I
was healthy enough to start receiving immunosuppressant

infusions, and I spent time learning to pace myself in occupational therapy.

When I was facing the challenge of leaving a secure, predictable career track, I was petrified I wouldn't be able to support myself or my family. I was raised to believe you never leave a job without an offer in hand and that a break in employment would make it impossible to find work in the future. The illness made those choices seem relatively unimportant but also crucial. It was terrifying living through this uncertainty, but, today, I live a life my twenty-one-year-old self would be proud of. Thirteen years into my marriage, my husband and I have worked hard to find the right balance for our family, my children are thriving, my clients provide accommodations for me to thrive, and my service dog, Peanut, helps me when I get triggered and need support.

I had the chance to sit down for lunch recently with a mentor of mine from my early days in tech who was going through a rough career patch. I shared with her that, although leaving corporate America was terrifying and I did not know how I was going to make enough money, nothing is worth the stress and the impact on your health. I shared with her that, since 2018, I have made more money each year, even though, when I was getting my company off the ground, I did not make any money for the first nine months. By betting on myself, the payoff was not only purpose, but also real security in knowing that I had marketable skills and a robust network. I confirmed that I would be okay no matter what challenges faced me next. It may be the gift of getting older, but I no longer fear feeling stuck. I now know how to recognize bad situations earlier, assess the landscape, and plan my exit and recovery plan more quickly.

I must have watched *The Wizard of Oz* a hundred times when I was a child. Some of its lessons I am rediscovering today from a new perspective. Just like Dorothy, only you have the power to find your way home. When the curtain is pulled back and the Wizard is revealed to be a fraud, he states: "You have plenty of courage, I am sure. All you need is confidence in yourself. There is no living thing that is not afraid when it faces danger. The true courage is in facing danger when you are afraid, and that kind of courage you have in plenty."

Through the career reboot process, you have faced your fears and overcome your objections to creating your own yellow brick road. Remember: no one has ever said, "I ignored my gut instinct and it turned out great!" Trust yourself and bet big on your dreams. It is never the things we tried that we regret; it is risks we never took that haunt us. It is never too late to start moving toward your own wisdom and to bust through the myths society has told you about what is possible for your future.

I no longer give my power away to the to the narcissists I have worked for or known socially. I finally learned the harsh lesson of how you can lose your sense of safety and security when you don't set and hold healthy boundaries. My husband, parents, children, therapist, and allies are there to help me put the pieces of myself back together after every setback. It has taken time to learn how to trust myself and to leave toxicity behind instead of hoping a situation will get better on its own. My hope for you, dear reader, is that you can be a quicker learner than I was. Embrace the opportunities ahead of you to live the life of your dreams. Thank you for coming along on my journey of learning how to recapture your personal happiness while defining your own career legacy.

Remembering Hasan

Mahmudul Hasan

n June 2022, Mahmudul Hasan, my business partner and one of my biggest supporters in writing a book, contracted COVID. Since he was vaccinated, young, and healthy, I was not too worried about it. We had planned to meet for dinner on Saturday, July 9, but he cancelled because he did not feel well. I was relieved; I was not feeling very well either. We rescheduled for coffee for Thursday, July 14. I was going to pick him up from a doctor's appointment and drive him home.

When I arrived at Kaiser, he didn't answer my text messages about which floor he was on. Eventually, I got frustrated and went inside. The receptionist directed me to the fourth floor. When I reached the fourth floor waiting room, a nurse said he would be transferred to another hospital, so I would not need to drive him home.

The next thing I knew, firemen and EMTs were rushed in, and Hasan came out on a stretcher. He looked dazed but calm. In the elevator, I let him know I was there, that he was not alone. He said he'd had a heart attack that morning. While they checked whether he was stable enough to transport, he had another heart attack on the ten-minute drive to the emergency room. They were able to stabilize him, and he was admitted to the ICU.

Even though I was at the same hospital for my infusions for five hours the next day, I was not allowed to visit him in the ICU because I was not family. We texted a lot over the next month as he was transferred to UCSF hospital and was kept in the ICU there. He had testing to decide whether he needed a heart transplant. After nearly thirty days, it was decided that his heart was in good shape, so they released him, with a bypass surgery scheduled in ninety days. He was home less than twenty-four hours before his third and final heart attack.

The last text I sent him was to say thank you for encouraging me to write this book. He replied with a heart emoji, and we made a phone appointment for 11:00 a.m. the next day to talk. I woke up in the morning to a text from his wife saying simply, "He's gone." He died forty-five minutes after he sent that heart emoji. I drove my kids to school and went straight to my parents' house because I could not bear to watch the clock turn 11:00 a.m. and know I could never pick up the phone and call him ever again.

His encouragement and support gave me the emotional energy to begin writing this book. Hasan, the world does not make as much sense without you in it, but today, I feel reborn in my new identity as an author. This is just one more gift you gave me before you left to rest in peace. Who would have guessed a Muslim boy from a chicken farm in Bangladesh and a Jewish girl from Detroit would come together to change the world? You are forever loved, my chosen brother.

Acknowledgments

To my fellow social justice warriors who have dedicated their time and knowledge to help bringing light to dark places, thank you. Specifically, Edward Dixon, Courtney Gregoire, Yiota Souras, Adrian Chandley, Tiffany Moeller, Bailey Danielson, Roo Powell, Travis Bright, Einat Clark, Emily Kennedy, Rachael Tyler, Lisa Perrone, Ken LeTourneau, John Sydow, Mike McCarter, Roopal McDuff, Federico Gomez Suarez, Nick Edmonds, Paige Johnson, Ray Bryant, Ashlie Bryant, Gregg Descheemaeker, Mahmudul Hasan, Genetha Gray, Lisa Davis, Teresa Herd, Justin Davis, Sheryl Tullis, Russ Whitman, Lee Christopherson, Kim Milbauer, Hilary DeCesare, Mary Mazzio, John Shehan, Stacia Shehan, Michelle DuLaune, Laura Horton, Will Ferrier, Jan Edwards, Matt Rosenquist, John Clark, Katrina Lyon-Smith, Diane Bryant, Gayle Sheppard, Bob Rogers, Julie Cordua, and Lakecia Gunter.

I started to write this book after reading *Finding Your Unicorn Space: A Woman's Guide to Reclaiming Your Creativity* by Eve Rodsky. I was effectively bedridden, and it was the only creative outlet I had left to try. A couple of months later, I shared a couple of chapters with Eve, and she was kind enough to introduce me to my publisher. A huge shoutout of thanks to Eve for helping me get this into print! Also, thank you to the authors and editors who provided guidance, encouragement, and inspiration: Brad Johnson, David Smith, Eve Rodsky, Jamie Fiore Higgins, Julia Goldstein, Michael Amato, Greg Larkin, Nicholas Boothman, Vikki Mueller Espinosa, Sandra Neihaus, Amii Bernard-Bahn, Carla Jones, Lisen Stromburg, Helen Horyaza, Mary Groethe, Prashant Natarajan, Shanta Mohan, Erin Carroll, Amanda Elysse Hughes, and Lee Reed Zarnikau.

Finally, I am forever grateful for my family's support. Thanks to my husband, Garrett, and my children, Tessa and Brandon. Thanks to my mom and dad, Suzanne and David Polvi, for making me go to engineering school, even if I did not like it at the time. Thanks also to Craig and Lynn Fraser for your support as grandparents in helping me to have the space and time to write and for being at all the kids' activities and being engaged in our family throughout this journey.

The Executive's Guide to Retaining Your Top Talent

The cost of employee turnover in the US is around $160 billion, according to Deloitte.[1] Beyond the monetary costs, lost employees also means lost time; full productivity is often delayed by three to six months for a new hire.[2] Starting another search can get expensive fast.

Many factors contribute to turnover, and it's not just salary and benefits. You may lose valuable employees because they do not feel like they belong in your company; this may be because no one else at the company looks like them, or it may be because they don't feel included. You may also lose crucial partners by working them out of the job. Once you have high performers that are also great leaders, it is important to pay attention to signs of burnout. You don't want to be caught flat-footed by the surprise departure of a key team member.

DIVERSITY

Greg Merrill, senior director of digital transformation at Nike, called diversity, equity, and inclusion "a business imperative for growth." Talent is evenly distributed, but the demographics of most US companies are not. A truly diverse workplace means diverse thoughts, which lead to new diverse ideas. Innovation doesn't exist without new ideas.

But hiring isn't enough. Being in the room doesn't necessarily mean included. When your team feels free to bring their entire self to work, they will bring creativity that will accelerate innovation. And that means increased revenue for your company. When we design for inclusion, everyone benefits.

Look in your own network. You will find promising people who may need your support. Believe in them, and help them lead. Below is a short exercise to taking steps toward increasing and supporting diversity on your team.

DIVERSE ALLY WORKSHEET

Can you share a time that someone attached their name to yours to give you access to an opportunity you might otherwise have had to prove yourself?

How did you meet that person?

Why do you think they took a chance on you?

Who is in your network that is deserving but lacking an opportunity to prove themselves?

What opportunity can you give that person to showcase their leadership?

What is the legacy you want to leave?

Once you have answered these questions please set up a coffee conversation with two people you have identified as potential talent for development. Start a quarterly rhythm for seeking their input on future directions and goals for the organizations, see if they help you fill in blind spots and are interested in being part of driving the new model going forward.

BURNOUT

As Asa Don Brown put it, when "an individual has experienced prolonged demands, chronic stress, fatigue, a lack of support, and a decreased satisfaction in what they are doing," they are about to burn out—or already have. This is not a rare issue. Microsoft found that almost half of the respondents to an employee survey said they were burnt out at work. That number was 53 percent for managers.[3] It's even worse for underrepresented groups.

For example, in the 2022 Women in the Workplace report, McKinsey found that "Forty-three percent of women leaders are burned out, compared to only 31 percent of men at their level." The lack of societal supports for mid- and senior-career working women adds pressure; when that pressure boils over, they are likely to quit the only part of their life they *can* quit: their job.

SUPPORTING YOUR TEAM

Support from the upper leadership is crucial to retaining marginalized workers. Some workers may need particular accommodations, such as for the variety of disabilities associated with long COVID. Safety is also crucial for every employee, including from harassment. Although retaliation for reporting harassment in the workplace is illegal, it is not uncommon. Your voice from the top shapes what behaviors your corporate culture finds unacceptable.

Mentors

You can also ensure that each team member has a mentor to guide them, make them feel welcome, and help them grow. Sadie St. Lawrence said that mentorship allows women to "be able to connect with each other and create a place that they can feel empowered to live their full purpose."

A 2022 survey showed that mentors can be a powerful means of retaining top talent. The results are laid out in figure A.1.

Managers

Front line managers are also key to retaining women. It has often been said that people don't quit their jobs, they quit their bosses. A *Forbes* article put it clearly: "Managers are essential

How did you build support?

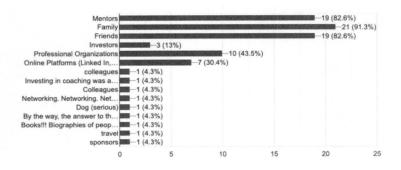

Figure A.1

drivers of workplace culture for all employees, and especially for women: Having a supportive manager is one of the top three factors women consider when deciding whether to join or stay with a company."[4]

Employee retention often pivots on how management treats their people. With authenticity, inclusion, and clarity—embodied at all levels of leadership—you will attract and retain the best workers.

Flexibility

We have lived through a couple of years of accelerated transformation in how we work. We now have data that flexible schedules and remote teams do not produce less productivity but enhance it. The future of work depends on us embracing this new model to keep more diverse perspectives in leadership and to move past antiquated ideas that face time in the office is what defines commitment.

Working parents need the flexibility to parent, and all of your employees should be trusted to manage their own time. That same *Forbes* article said that "Employees who can choose how they work best—whether remote or on-site—are less burned out, happier in their jobs, and much less likely to consider leaving their companies."[5]

To retain your top talent, it is important that you make promotion decisions based on results, not face time. It is important to notice when stigma is being applied to someone for a flexible work structure, which is more likely to be taken advantage of by women. It is important to break that bias that a remote or flexible work arrangement is correlated with being less committed or productive. We now have years of data to support the fact that that is a bias and not an accurate reflection of the workforce.

ACT FAST

In a 2022 survey I conducted of women in C-suite leadership roles, I learned that once they decided they need to go, burnt out employees act quickly. You can see the numbers in figure A.2. The respondents were asked when they felt it was time to blow up their career with a drastic change.

Once they were ready to make a change, the move happened pretty quickly; you don't have a lot of time to change their minds. The big message for execs here is that an ounce of prevention is worth a pound of cure. You will lose access to best innovation unless your company creates a space for the best innovators. You need those innovators to choose your

How long did it take you to take action on that feeling?

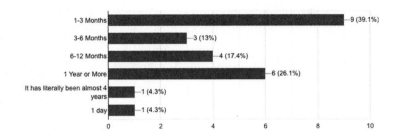

Figure A.2

company—not just to join your team but to stay on it. That means you need to nurture their opportunities for growth and demonstrate an investment in that vision. And it means a diverse, safe, and flexible workplace.

Notes

PREFACE

1. Margie Warrell, "Women Are Quitting: How We Can Curb the 'She-Cession' and Support Working Women," *Forbes*, January 6, 2021, https://www.forbes.com/sites/margiewarrell/2021/01/06/does-a-she-cession-loom-how-to-better-support-women-through-this-pandemic/?sh=71b2638f3ece.

2. Liz Elting, "The She-Cession by the Numbers," *Forbes*, February 12, 2022, https://www.forbes.com/sites/lizelting/2022/02/12/the-she-cession-by-the-numbers/?sh=2fe7cd2a1053.

3. Rachel Thomas et al., *Women in the Workplace 2021*, McKinsey & Company, 2021, https://wiw-report.s3.amazonaws.com/Women_in_the_Workplace_2021.pdf.

CHAPTER 2

1. US Bureau of Labor Statistics, "Labor Force Statistics from the Current Population Survey," Data extracted on December 1, 2022, https://data.bls.gov/timeseries/LNU02096055.

2. *Preventing Crimes against Children: Assessing the Legal Landscape: Hearing before the U.S. House of Representatives Subcommittee on Crime, Terrorism, Homeland Security, and Investigations of the Committee on the Judiciary,* March 16, 2017, (testimony of John Shehan, The National Center for Missing and Exploited Children).

CHAPTER 3

1. Alistair Carmichael, Erica Hutchins Coe, and Martin
   Dewhurst, "Employee Mental health and Burnout in Asia:
   A Time to Act," McKinsey.com blog, August 18, 2022,
   https://www.mckinsey.com/featured-insights/future-of-asia/
   employee-mental-health-and-burnout-in-asia-a-time-to-act.

2. Caroline Mimbs Nyce, "The Cure for Burnout Is Not Self-Care," the
   Atlantic, September 13, 2022, https://www.theatlantic.com/ideas/
   archive/2022/09/what-is-quiet-quitting-burnout-at-work/671413/.

CHAPTER 4

1. Lara Bull-Otterson, et al., "Post-COVID Conditions among Adult
   COVID-19 Survivors Aged 18–64 and ≥ 65 Years—United States,
   March 2020–November 2021," *CDC Weekly*, May 27, 2022, 71(21);
   pages 713–717, https://www.cdc.gov/mmwr/volumes/71/wr/
   mm7121e1.htm.

2. Spencer Kimball, "U.S. Scientists Enroll Nearly 40,000 Patients in
   High-Stakes, $1.2 Billion Study of Long COVID," CNBC.com,
   updated July 9, 2022, https://www.cnbc.com/2022/07/08/long-
   covid-us-scientists-to-enroll-40000-in-1point2-billion-study-.html.

3. Kimball, "U.S. Scientists Enroll Nearly 40,000 Patients."

CHAPTER 5

1. "16 Alarming Sexual Harassment in the Workplace
   Statistics You Need to Know," Inspired eLearning (blog),
   July 12, 2021, https://inspiredelearning.com/blog/
   sexual-harassment-in-the-workplace-statistics/.

2. Phil Mattingly and Maegan Vazquez, "Biden Signs Bill overhauling
   Workplace Sexual Misconduct Into Law," *CNN* online, March 3,
   2022, updated 6:32 p.m. EST, https://www.cnn.com/2022/03/03/
   politics/biden-sexual-misconduct-bill-signing/index.html.

3. Phil Mattingly and Maegan Vazquez, "Biden signs bill overhauling workplace sexual misconduct into law," *CNN*, March 3, 2022, https://www.cnn.com/2022/03/03/politics/biden-sexual-misconduct-bill-signing/index.html.
4. Kasia Urbaniak, "Can't Speak Up? It's Not a Lack of Confidence. It's the Freeze," Kasia Urbaniak (blog), February 14, 2020, https://www.kasiaurbaniak.com/blog/women-with-confidence-break-the-freeze.

CHAPTER 7

1. Robin Hauser, "The Likability Dilemma for Women Leaders," TED, April 13, 2022, https://www.ted.com/talks/robin_hauser_the_likability_dilemma_for_women_leaders_may_2022?language=en#:~:text=When%20women%20lead%2C%20bias%20often,to%20be%20a%20good%20leader.
2. Alexis Krivkovich et al., "Women in the Workplace 2022," McKinsey & Company, October 18, 2022, https://www.mckinsey.com/featured-insights/diversity-and-inclusion/women-in-the-workplace.

CHAPTER 8

1. Courtney Connley, "Gates Foundation Commits $2.1 Billion Over the Next Five Years to Gender Equality," *CNN* online blog, June 30, 2021, https://www.cnbc.com/2021/06/30/gates-foundation-commits-2point1-billion-to-gender-equality-over-next-5-years.html.
2. Marian Wright Edelman, "It's Hard To Be What You Can't See," *Child Watch Column* (blog), Children's Defense Fund, August 21, 2015, https://www.childrensdefense.org/child-watch-columns/health/2015/its-hard-to-be-what-you-cant-see.
3. Suzette Hackney, "Melinda French Gates: Courage Is 'Using Your Voice' to Push for Necessary but Controversial Change," *USA Today*, March 13, 2022, updated May 3, 2022, https://www.usatoday.com/in-depth/opinion/2022/03/13/melinda-french-gates-usa-today-women-of-the-year-2022/6844222001/.

4. "What Is Intersectionality," Center for Intersectional Justice, https://www.intersectionaljustice.org/what-is-intersectionality.

CHAPTER 9

1. Thomas L. Rodziewicz, Benjamin Houseman, John E. Hipskind, "Medical Error Reduction and Prevention," (StatPearls, 2022), https://www.ncbi.nlm.nih.gov/books/NBK499956.

2. Edwin Leap, "Reporting From the Healthcare Disaster," Life and Limb (blog), https://edwinleap.substack.com/p/reporting-from-the-healthcare-disaster.

3. Leap, "Reporting From the Healthcare Disaster."

CHAPTER 10

1. Lisa Thee and Gregg Descheemaeker, "Male Allies Help Make My Entrepreneurial Dreams a Reality. Here's How . . .," LinkedIn, November 20, 2019, https://www.linkedin.com/pulse/male-allies-helped-make-my-entrepreneurial-dreams-how-thee-polvi-.

CHAPTER 11

1. Edward Segal, "New Surveys Show Burnout Is an International Crisis," *Forbes*, October 15, 2022, https://www-forbes-com.cdn.ampproject.org/c/s/www.forbes.com/sites/edwardsegal/2022/10/15/surveys-show-burnout-is-an-international-crisis/amp/.

2. Jessica Ourisman, "Breathwork Has Gone Mainstream During the COVID Era," *Harper's Bazaar*, February 5, 2021, https://www.harpersbazaar.com/beauty/health/a35395134/what-is-breathwork/.

3. Barb Carr, "Live Your Core Values: 10-Minute Exercise to Increase Your Success," TapRoot, April 11, 2013, https://www.taproot.com/live-your-core-values-exercise-to-increase-your-success.

4. Marie Leech, "The Million-Dollar Mistake: Women Fall Short When Negotiating Salaries," *bizwomen, The Business Journals*, July 28, 2022, https://www.bizjournals.com/bizwomen/news/profiles-strategies/2022/07/the-million-dollar-mistake-women-fall-short-on.html?page=all.

CHAPTER 14

1. Brianna Wiest, "61% of Women Are Planning a Major Career Change Post-Pandemic, New Survey Shows," *Forbes*, September 8, 2020, https://www.forbes.com/sites/briannawiest/2020/09/08/61-of-women-are-planning-a-major-career-change-post-pandemic-new-survey-shows/?sh=4e029a08417c.

2. Camille Kapaun, "The Illusion of Venture Capital for Female Founders," *Forbes*, June 21, 2022, https://www.forbes.com/sites/columbiabusinessschool/2022/06/21/the-illusion-of-venture-capital-for-female-founders/?sh=10d1367474c6.

APPENDIX

1. John Bersin, "Employee Retention Now a Big Issue: Why the Tide Has Turned," LinkedIn, August 16, 2013, https://www.linkedin.com/pulse/20130816200159-131079-employee-retention-now-a-big-issue-why-the-tide-has-turned.

2. Gennaro Cuofano, "Tuckman's Model of Group Development in a Nutshell," FourWeekMBA (November 29, 2022), https://fourweekmba.com/tuckmans-model-of-group-development.

3. Edward Segal, "New Surveys Show Burnout Is an International Crisis," *Forbes*, October 15, 2022, https://www-forbes-com.cdn.ampproject.org/c/s/www.forbes.com/sites/edwardsegal/2022/10/15/surveys-show-burnout-is-an-international-crisis/amp.

4. Holly Corbett, "The 'Great Breakup' and Why Women Leaders Are Leaving Companies at Higher Rates," *Forbes*, October 18, 2022, https://www.forbes.com/sites/hollycorbett/2022/10/18/the-great-breakup-and-why-women-leaders-are-leaving-companies-at-higher-rates/?sh=6744339e43d7.

5. Corbett, "The 'Great Breakup.'"

About the Author

Lisa Thee is a Top 50 Global Thought Leader for AI, Privacy, Cybersecurity, and Safety, with demonstrated experience in delivering revenue and solving complex business technology, governance, privacy, and risk challenges at scale.

Mrs. Thee is a consultant to some of the world's most innovative healthcare and global technology companies, including Microsoft and UCSF's Center for Digital Healthcare Innovation, helping to accelerate FDA approval for AI use in clinical settings. She was the CEO and cofounder of Minor Guard, an artificial intelligence software company focused on making people safer online and in real life. She is a keynote speaker, including her TEDx talk "Bringing Light to Dark Places Online: Disrupting Human Trafficking Using AI." She hosts the award-winning *Navigating Forward* podcast. She was named to the 2022 Top Health and Safety, Privacy, and AI Thought Leaders and Influencers and Women in Business you should follow by Thinkers360. She was also named to the 2022 Top 100 Brilliant Women in AI Ethics global list and to the Top 10 Impactful Women in Cybersecurity from *Woman Achiever* magazine.

Mrs. Thee currently serves as an advisory board member for Engineered Medical Solutions and Spectrum Labs. She is also a board of directors member for Humaxa, an HR-focused AI software company, and for 3Strands Global Foundation, an organization focused on human trafficking prevention and reintegration. As CEO and chairman of the board for Minor Guard, she secured seed funding, led product development, and set the sales strategy. She brings board value for ESG, specifically around AI ethics and diversity and inclusion.

Mrs. Thee has nineteen years of digital director experience, most recently overseeing $6 billion in business for Intel's data center and storage markets. Mrs. Thee led engagements for big data solutions to disrupt child exploitation in partnership with the National Center for Missing and Exploited Children, Google, and Microsoft, including ingestion, transition to hybrid cloud, and building machine learning models to accelerate the coordinated national response to child abuse reports from thirty days to twenty-four hours. As the founder of the project, she secured $4 million in funding for hardware and engineering resources for 2017.

Mrs. Thee holds a bachelor of science in industrial and operations management engineering, from the University of Michigan. She is also a certified project management professional who has been licensed by the Project Management Institute since 2005.